The REPUBLIC and The LAWS

Cicero
(Translated by Niall Rudd)

Teacher Guide

Michelle Luoma

MEMORIA PRESS

www.MemoriaPress.com

THE REPUBLIC & THE LAWS
Cicero (Translated by Niall Rudd)

TEACHER GUIDE
Michelle Luoma

ISBN 978-1-61538-352-8

First Edition © 2013 Memoria Press

CONTENTS

THE
REPUBLIC

THE REPUBLIC SYNOPSIS

BOOK 1

1-13 Preface

fr. Obligations of the individual to the state

fr. Importance of both experience and theoretical education

2-12 Anti-Epicureanism: refuting arguments against political engagement

13 Cicero's experience and learning as qualifications for writing

14-37 Introductory Conversation

14-18 The social gathering and the double sun

19-26 The value of astronomy

26-30 Philosophy as both perspective and practical preparation

31-37 The main subject: the best form of republic

38-71 Constitutional Theory

38-42 The origins of society and simple constitutions

43-45 Disadvantages of simple constitutions and advantages of mixed forms

46-50 The argument for democracy

51-53 The argument for aristocracy

54-55 Advantages of simple constitutions, Scipio prefers monarchy

56-64 The argument for monarchy, the gods and the universe (56-57),

history (58), the mind (59-60), the structure of the household (61), expediency in a

crisis (62-63), the people love kings (64)

65-69 The instability and corruptibility of simple constitutions, the advantages of mixed constitutions

70-71 Conclusion: Rome's constitution as the best constitution

BOOK 2

1-3 Preface: Comparison between Roman and Greek governments

4-20 Romulus

4 Birth and childhood

4-9 Choosing the site

10-11 Founding Rome

12-13 The Sabines and Titus Tatius

14-16 Establishing the senate and auspices

17-20 Apotheosis

21-52 Early Kings

21-22 Plato, the Peripatetics, and Scipio

23-30 Numa

23-24 Interregnum

25 Election

26-7 Numa's reign

28-30 Numa and Pythagoras

BOOK 5: The Statesman

BOOK 6: The Dream of Scipio

READING GUIDE

Lesson I	Book 1.1-13
Lesson II	Book 1.14-37
Lesson III	Book 1.38-50
Lesson IV	Book 1.51-71
Lesson V	Book 2.1-20
Lesson VI	Book 2.21-36
Lesson VII	Book 2.37-70
Lesson VIII	Book 3.1-28
Lesson IX	Book 3.29-46
Lesson X	Books 4 and 5
Lesson XI	Book 6

THE REPUBLIC

Book 1

LESSON I: The Republic, Book 1.1-13

TEACHING NOTES

Homework Questions: 3, 4, 5, 6, 7, 9, 10, 12, 13, 14, 15

Quiz Questions: 4, 7, 9, 10, 13, 14

Discussion Focus Questions: 1

SYNOPSIS

Book 1.1-13 Preface

fr. Obligations of the individual to the state

fr. Importance of both experience and theoretical education

2-12 Anti-Epicureanism: refuting arguments against political engagement

13 Cicero's experience and learning as qualifications for writing

I. THOUGHT QUESTIONS:

1. Which do you think is more important preparation for writing political philosophy, experience or education?

II. COMPREHENSION QUESTIONS:

1. What overcomes all enticements of pleasure and ease?

   1.1

   Nature has given men a need for virtue and a desire to defend the common safety.

2. What is virtue and what is it not?

   1.2

   Virtue is not some kind of knowledge to be possessed without using it. It consists entirely in its use.

   Note: *This is a peripatetic view.*

3. What is the most important use of virtue?

   1.2

   The most important use of virtue is the governance of states and the accomplishment in deeds rather than words of the things about which philosophers talk.

4. Why is law superior to philosophy?

   1.3

   The law compels everyone to do what philosophy can persuade only a few people to do.

5. Why are statesmen superior to philosophers?

   1.3

   Just as cities are superior to villages, men who lead cities should be considered far wiser than philosophers who have no experience of public life.

6. What causes men to be eager to make human life better and safer?

   1.3

   Nature itself

7. List the arguments made against taking part in public life in sections 4-6, and Cicero's refutation of each.
    1.4-6

    Note: *Epicurus recommended avoiding politics, but many Romans were both Epicureans and politicians.*

    - The labor it takes to defend the commonwealth: It is a minor burden for an alert and vigorous man.
    - The danger to one's life (supported by examples of political/military disasters such as Miltiades or Themistocles): To fear death is disgraceful. Death is inevitable, and it is far more miserable to be worn away by nature and old age than to lay down one's life for one's country.
    - The danger of exile, including Cicero's exile as an example: Those who make these arguments also went overseas during the civil wars.

8. What does Cicero list as false claims about why the country gives birth to its citizens?
    1.8

    To serve our convenience or provide a safe refuge for our relaxation and a quiet place for rest.

9. What claim does Cicero assert a country makes on its citizens?
    1.8

    She has a claim on the largest and best part of our minds, talents, loyalty, and judgment for her own use, and leaves us for our private use only so much as is beyond her requirements.

10. List the arguments made against taking part in public life in sections 9-10, and Cicero's refutation of each.
    1.9-10

    - Those who take part in public life are worthless men; to be paired with them is low, and to fight against them is dangerous.
    - Good and brave men should not allow themselves to be subject to wicked men or allow wicked men to ravage the commonwealth while they are capable of helping it.
    - A wise man will take no part in public affairs unless a crisis compels him. It is impossible to bring aid to the state in a crisis if you are not already in a position to do so.

11. Why does Cicero believe that philosophers should not neglect knowledge of public administration?
    1.11

    They ought to prepare in advance for whatever they might need.

12. What does Cicero state is his goal in writing *De Re Publica*?

1.12

His goal is to provide a discussion of the state and to advocate involvement in it.

13. Why does Cicero believe that classical philosophers who did not hold office perform an important public function?

1.12

They did much research and writing about government.

14. What human virtue does Cicero believe most closely approaches the divine?

1.12

Founding new states or preserving existing ones.

15. Why does Cicero believe he should be considered an authority on his topic?

1.13

Some earlier figures were skilled in argument but performed no public actions, while others were admirable in deeds but poor in exposition. Cicero has achieved something memorable in his public career and has a capacity for explaining the principles of civic life.

LESSON II: The Republic, Book 1.14-37

TEACHING NOTES

Homework Questions: Memorize all participants in the dialogue, 1, 2, 3, 5, 7, 11, 12, 13, 14, 15, 16, 17, 18, 19, 20, 23, 24, 25, 27, 28, 29

Quiz Questions: participants in the dialogue, 11, 12, 15, 16, 17, 18, 19, 20, 28

Discussion Focus Questions: 1, 2, 4

SYNOPSIS

Book 1.14-37 Introductory Conversation

14-18 The social gathering and the double sun

19-26 The value of astronomy

26-30 Philosophy as both perspective and practical preparation

31-37 The main subject: the best form of republic

I. THOUGHT QUESTIONS:

1. What do you believe is the value of philosophy?

2. Are some philosophical pursuits greater than others?

3. Are those educated in philosophy better prepared to take up the administration of the state than those who are not?

4. Does education imply greater obligation to the state?

5. What do you think is the value of astronomy or of scientific inquiry?

> *"But what element of human affairs should a man think*
> *glorious who has examined this kingdom of the gods;*
> *or long-lived who has learned what eternity really is; or*
> *glorious who has seen how small the earth is—first the*
> *whole earth, then that part of it which men inhabit?"*
>
> *- De Re Publica 1.26*

II. PARTICIPANTS IN THE DIALOGUE:

Scipio: Scipio Aemilianus, the destroyer of Carthage, an extraordinary general who did not threaten the state as the great generals of Cicero's time did. He was known to patronize writers. In the dialogue, he appears as an idealist and theoretician, much like Cicero himself. Do not confuse him with his grandfather, Scipio Africanus, whom we shall encounter in Book 6.

Laelius: Laelius Sapiens, a friend of Scipio's; politically cautious, practical, and down-to-earth

Manilius: a legal expert

Philus: a man of great personal rectitude who nevertheless takes on the defense of injustice for the sake of argument

Mummius: conservative, anti-democracy

Tubero: Scipio's nephew and an eager student of philosophy

Rutilius: a young participant in the dialogue

Fannius: a young participant in the dialogue

Scaevola: a young participant in the dialogue

III. COMPREHENSION QUESTIONS:

1. What is Tubero's question that opens the philosophical dialogue?

   1.15

   What is the meaning of the second sun that has been seen in the Senate?

2. How does Scipio respond to Tubero's question?

   1.15

   He says that Socrates was wiser for giving up all concerns of this sort (signs and portents), and for saying that natural philosophy seeks either things greater than human understanding, or things that have nothing to do with human existence.

3. How does Tubero refute this?

   1.16

   He reminds them that Socrates linked morals, virtues, and public life to numbers, geometry, and harmony in the manner of Pythagoras.

4. Who does Cicero claim is his informant about this dialogue?

   1.17

   Publius Rutilius

5. What was the arrangement of friendship between Laelius and Scipio?

    1.18

    Laelius would treat Scipio almost like a god when they were on campaign because of
    his military prowess, and that in Rome, Scipio treated Laelius like a father because he
    was older.

6. How does Laelius's question in 1.19 reveal his character?

    1.19

    He asks whether the participants are so informed about things that concern the res
    publica and their homes that they have to inquire about what is going on in the sky,
    revealing his common sense, practical approach to philosophy.

7. How does Philus respond from a Stoic perspective?

    1.19

    Philus says the home of mankind is the whole universe, which is shared with the gods.

8. Why does Philus think investigating the portent of the double sun is worthwhile?

    1.19

    The investigation of such things brings pleasure to all those eager for wisdom.

9. What is that branch of learning that Manilius defends as the one without which no one can know what
   is his own and what is someone else's?

    1.20

    The law

10. Why is Philus impressed with Archimedes' globe?

    1.22

    Archimedes had discovered how a single turning action could preserve the unequal
    orbits with their different speeds.

11. Why was Scipio impressed by Galus?

1.23

Galus had been able to convince the troops to set aside their fear at an eclipse by explaining it as a natural and scientific phenomenon rather than a portent of ill luck from the gods.

1.24

"He relieved those desperately worried soldiers from groundless superstition and fear. That was a highly important feat."

12. Who does Scipio say was the first to recognize eclipses?

1.25

Thales of Miletus

13. What does Cicero assert is the value of astronomy in 1.19-1.26, and what does that tell us about Cicero?

1.25

Scientific explanation allows men to function rationally by dispelling religious fear. This reveals Cicero's skepticism.

14. Who does Scipio believe is fortunate, and why?

1.27

Scipio asserts that a man is fortunate who is not accustomed to believing anything is his possession. He is fortunate because he alone can truly claim all things as his own.

15. Who does Scipio believe is the worst kind of person?

1.27

Often the worst kind of person has possessions and power in limitless quantities.

Note: *The tension between Cicero's aristocratic bias and his accompanying disdain for the plebes (which reveals itself more in the Laws), and the Roman value of austerity and distrust of wealth and luxury as weakening influences, will continue throughout his works.*

One of the goals of this course is to help students think critically, and in a nuanced manner. Encourage students to understand these perspectives as both quintessentially Roman patrician viewpoints, rather than giving in to the temptation to oversimplify and dismiss Cicero as self-contradictory. If they have trouble with this, point out similar tensions in American society and values.

16. How does Scipio define the common law of nature regarding possessions?

1.27

It forbids anything to belong to anyone except someone who knows how to employ and use it.

17. Who does Scipio say is the wealthiest man?

1.28

The wealthiest man lacks nothing of what nature requires.

18. Who does Scipio say is the most powerful man?

1.28

The most powerful man achieves all that he seeks.

19. Who does Scipio say is the most blessed man?

1.28

The most blessed man is the man who is freed from emotional disturbance.

Note: *This is a Stoic idea.*

20. Who does Scipio say is the man of the most secure good fortune?

1.28

The man who possesses only what he can carry with him out of a shipwreck is of the most secure good fortune. (i.e., the man who has few possessions)

21. What does Scipio say is grander than any power, office, or kingdom?

1.28

To look down on all things human and to think of them as less important than wisdom, and to turn over in his mind nothing except what is eternal and divine is grander than any power, office, or kingdom.

22. Who does Scipio say are the only true humans?

1.28

The only true humans are those who have been educated in truly human arts.

23. What does Scipio apparently believe is the purpose of philosophy as revealed in sections 1.26-1.29?

Philosophy's function is to provide proper perspective on human affairs.

24. What studies does Laelius say are more suitable to free men and more widely applicable?

1.30

Those which address the needs of practical life.

25. What does Laelius say is the value of philosophy?

1.30

If philosophy has any value, it is that they sharpen and stimulate the minds of the young so that they can learn greater things more easily.

26. What things does Laelius believe are greater topics for conversation than philosophy?

1.31-1.32

Laelius is perturbed about the politically divided republic, and believes that while it is not possible to truly know the meaning of two suns, it is possible to reunite the Senate and the people, which will result in better and happier lives.

27. What does Laelius say is the most outstanding task of philosophy as well as the greatest evidence and function of virtue?

1.33

The skills that make us useful to the state.

28. What does Laelius say Scipio believed to be the best condition of the state?

1.34

The condition handed down by the ancestors.

29. What is Scipio's ancestral craft?

1.35

The administration of the state: "the supervision and management of the country."

LESSON III: The Republic, Book 1.38-50

TEACHING NOTES

Homework Questions: 2, 4, 7, 9, 11, 12, 14, 15, 16, 17, 20, 21, 22, 24, 25, 26, 30, 31, 32, 33, 34

Quiz Questions: 7, 12, 20, 26, 30, 31

Discussion Focus Questions: 1, Comprehension Question #9

SYNOPSIS

Book 1.38-71 Constitutional Theory

38-42 The origins of society and simple constitutions

43-45 Disadvantages of simple constitutions and advantages of mixed forms

46-50 The argument for democracy

I. THOUGHT QUESTIONS:

1. Do you think differences in status have the potential to undermine a state, as Scipio describes in section 1.49? Why or why not?

2. What do you think are the origins of civilization? Why do you think humans first grouped together?

II. COMPREHENSION QUESTIONS:

1. What does Scipio say needs to be done before any speaker on any subject should speak, to avoid mistakes?

   1.38

   All should agree on the subject under discussion and explain what is signified by that name.

2. How does Scipio define a republic?

   1.39

   A republic is the property of the public.

   Note: *Section 39 is basically an Aristotelian approach.*

3. How does Scipio define a people?

   1.39

   A people is an assemblage of some size associate with one another through agreement on law and community of interest.

4. Why does Scipio say people first assembled?

   1.39

   Through a natural herding together rather than through weakness.

5. In the quote from Lactantius, why does he say people first assembled?

   1.40

   They herded together because the nature of humans shuns solitude and seeks community and society.

6. What does Scipio say was the first act of assembled men?

   1.41

   To establish a settlement in a fixed location for their homes.

7. Describe an early town and an early city in Scipio's model.

   1.41

   town: consists of homes protected by fortifications

   city: a town which includes shrines and common spaces

8. How does Scipio define a state?

   1.41

   The organization of the people

9. What does Scipio say every state and every republic needs in order to be long-lived?

1.41

Every state and republic needs to be ruled by some sort of deliberation which is connected to the original cause of the formation of the state.

10. What forms does Scipio say deliberation must take?

1.42

It must be assigned to one person or to selected individuals or taken up by the entire population.

11. What makes any form of government tolerable for Scipio?

1.42

It is tolerable if it holds to the bond which first bound men together in the association of a commonwealth.

12. Which form of government does Scipio say is least desirable?

1.42

Rule by the people

13. According to Scipio, what can prevent any form of government from existing in a stable condition?

1.42

Wickedness and greed

Note: *This can also be translated as "injustice and greed."*

14. What does Scipio say is the downfall of monarchies?

1.43

The people play too small a part in the community's legislation and debate.

15. What does Scipio say is the downfall of oligarchies?

1.43

The people hardly have any share in liberty because they lack any role in discussion and decision making.

16. What does Scipio say is the downfall of democracies?

1.43

No matter how just a democracy may be, Scipio maintains that equality is inequitable because it involves no degrees of merit.

Note: *This can also be translated as "degrees of status."*

17. What example does Scipio use for the downside of each form of government?

1.43

Monarchy: Cyrus the Great of Persia was just and wise, but that is hardly consistent with Scipio's definition of a state as the "concern of the people."

Oligarchy: The people of Massilia/Marseilles are ruled justly but are basically enslaved.

Democracy: The Athenians did not maintain the splendor of the state because there were not degrees of status.

18. What does Scipio say is the part of a wise man?

1.45

To recognize the cycles of changes in governments.

19. What does Scipio say is the part of a truly great citizen and nearly divine man?

1.45

To anticipate changes and keep the course of the state under his control.

20. What kind of government does Scipio say is most to be desired?

1.45

One that is blended from the three basic types (monarchy, oligarchy, democracy).

21. What does Scipio say determines the character of a state?

1.47

The character and will of its ruling power.

22. According to Scipio, what is the only kind of state in which there can be liberty?

1.47

One in which the people has the highest power (democracy).

23. According to Scipio, what is sweeter than liberty?

1.47

Nothing

24. According to Scipio, what does liberty absolutely require?

1.47

Equality

25. Describe the duties of the citizens Scipio calls free in name only.

1.47

They vote, entrust commands and offices, are canvassed and asked for their support, and are asked to give what they do not have themselves.

26. What would they need to be free, and why are they not?

1.47

They would need political power, political voice, and judiciary power, but these things are apportioned on the basis of birth or wealth.

27. How does oligarchy or despotism come into being from democracy?

1.48

"... when one or more exceptionally rich and prosperous men emerge from the populace," arrogance and contempt lead to oligarchy or despotism because "the faint-hearted and the weak give way and succumb to the haughtiness of wealth."

28. What happens when people hold fast to their rights?

1.48

They are superior in power, liberty, and happiness, because they are in charge of laws, courts, war, peace, treaties, individual lives, and wealth.

29. Why is democracy the only form of government that deserves to be called a republic?

1.48

Democracy is the only form of government that deserves to be called a republic because freedom is restored from the domination of a king or senate, whereas kings or aristocrats are not summoned to take over from free peoples.

30. How does discord arise in a state?

1.49

It arises from incompatible interests, when different policies suit different people.

31. What holds a community of citizens together?

1.49

Equality under the law

32. What is the only question for the people under monarchy?

1.50

Whether they are the slaves of a kind or harsh master.

33. Why could Sparta not be sure of enjoying good and just kings?

1.50

It was obliged to accept as king whoever was born into a royal family.

34. On what criteria is a man to be judged "the best" (and ergo suitable for aristocracy)?

1.50

On the basis of his learning, his skills, and his activities.

LESSON IV: The Republic, Book 1.51-71

TEACHING NOTES

Homework Questions: 2, 4, 5, 6, 7, 10, 13, 14, 15, 19, 24, 27, 31, 32, 33, 34, 36

Quiz Questions: 10, 13, 14, 15, 24, 31

Discussion Focus Questions: 3, 1

SYNOPSIS

Book 1.51-53 The argument for aristocracy

54-55 Advantages of simple constitutions, Scipio prefers monarchy

56-64 The argument for monarchy, the gods and the universe (56-57),
history (58), the mind (59-60), the structure of the household (61), expediency in a
crisis (62-63), the people love kings (64)

65-69 The instability and corruptibility of simple constitutions, the advantages of mixed constitutions

70-71 Conclusion: Rome's constitution as the best constitution

I. THOUGHT QUESTIONS:

1. Scipio seems to believe that some people are just naturally better than others, and to treat everyone
equally is, then, unfair. Do you agree with Scipio's assessment of the stratification of human goodness?
Why or why not? **Note:** This is not based on a man's actions, but on his nature.

2. Do you agree with Scipio that equal treatment can lead to inequality or injustice? Why or why not?

3. Much of Scipio's support for monarchy rests on his implicit assumption that leading the state is a
specialized task that requires specialists (hence, the doctor and captain analogy), and therefore cannot
be properly carried out by anyone else. Do you agree? Why or why not?

II. COMPREHENSION QUESTIONS:

1. What does Scipio say will happen if a state leaves the election to office to chance?

   1.51

   The state will be "overturned as quickly as a ship in which a man chosen by lot from among the passengers has taken over the helm."

2. How does Scipio believe people should select aristocrats?

   1.51

   - A free people should choose them.
   - They should only choose the best men.
   - They should choose with a genuine desire for security.

3. What does Scipio assert nature has decreed regarding aristocracy?

   1.51

   Not only should men of superior character and ability be in charge of the less endowed, but also the latter should willingly obey their superiors.

4. What does Scipio call a "vulgar misconception" about aristocracy?

   1.51

   Aristocrats are those with large fortunes and possessions or who belong to famous families.

5. What happens as a result of that misconception?

   1.51

   A few with money rather than worth have gained control of the state. "Money, name, and property, if divorced from good sense and skill ... lapse into total degradation and supercilious insolence."

6. What does Scipio say is the most degenerate kind of state?

   1.52

   One in which the richest are thought to be the best.

7. What does Scipio say is the most splendid kind of state?

1.52

The most splendid kind of state is a state governed by worth, where the leader lives by the values he espouses, where the leader is subject to the law, and where the leader's life is an example of good conduct.

8. According to Scipio, why has authority been transferred from kings to larger groups?

1.52

Because of the difficulty of initiating policies.

9. According to Scipio, why has authority been transferred from the masses to the few?

1.52

Because of the bad judgment and recklessness of popular bodies.

10. What does Scipio say is always a risk?

1.53

That equality before the law cannot be maintained indefinitely, which causes the people to complain that their interests are being ignored by the leaders.

11. Why does Scipio say that equality is inequitable?

1.53

"... when the same respect is accorded to the highest and the lowest (who must be present in every nation), equity itself is most unequal."

12. Which simple form of government does Scipio prefer?

1.54

Monarchy, because it is like fatherhood.

13. Why does Scipio say it is hard to choose which system of government is best?

1.55

- Kings attract us by affection.
- Aristocracies attract us by good sense.
- Democracies attract us by freedom.

14. Why does Scipio assert that religion support monarchy?

1.56

He says there is one king in heaven who is regarded as the king and father of all, and all gods are ruled by one divine power.

15. Who do the Greeks say are barbarians?

1.58

All people other than Greeks.

16. What does Laelius assert has greater force than witnesses on any good judge?

1.59

Arguments

17. What does Scipio say there is no room for if reason is supreme in the mind?

1.60

Lust for power and glory, anger, irresponsible behavior.

18. What does Laelius say is the vilest thing in creation?

1.60

The sort of mind where reason has been replaced by anger and lust, and the person with that sort of mind.

19. Explain how the analogy of the ship's captain and the doctor supports monarchy.

1.62

If they are qualified in their professions, a ship would be entrusted to the captain alone, and an invalid to a doctor alone.

20. According to Scipio, why is the name of kings anathema to the Romans?

1.62

Because of the overbearing and arrogant nature of Tarquin alone.

21. Why does Scipio think more power is given to the people in times of peace and security?

1.63

You can act irresponsibly when you have nothing to be afraid of.

22. To what does Scipio compare people deprived of a just king?

1.64

Orphans

23. According to Scipio, what does monarchy turn into, and why?

1.65

It turns into tyranny because of injustice.

24. What does Scipio say is the worst kind of government?

1.65

Tyranny

25. According to Scipio, what does that form of government turn into, and why?

1.65

It turns into aristocracy because aristocrats overthrow tyrants.

26. How does Scipio say aristocracy is somewhat like monarchy?

1.65

It is a paternal council of leading men who have the best interests of the people at heart.

27. What does Scipio say happens when people depose a tyrant?

1.65-1.67

The people will behave with restraint and preserve the constitution they have set up.

28. What does Scipio say happens when people depose a just king or aristocracy?

1.65-1.67

They will condemn as tyrants any magistrates who do not give them freedom
generously. It eventually becomes anarchy.

29. From where does Scipio say the death of an aristocracy comes?

1.68

Its own excessive power.

30. What does Scipio say freedom does to an over-free populace?

1.68

It plunges it into slavery.

31. What does Scipio say turns any rule into its opposite?

1.68

Excess

32. Describe the leader chosen by Scipio's "excessively free" populace.

1.68

- He is brazen and dirty.
- He impudently harasses servants of the state.
- He gives property to the people.
- He is given powers because he faces threats.
- He is surrounded by a bodyguard.
- He tyrannizes the people.

Note: *Cicero is almost certainly making a reference to Caesar and/or the dictators.*

33. What happens if that leader is overthrown by decent citizens?

1.68

Constitutional government is restored.

Note: *This is not what happened in the case of Caesar.*

34. How does a junta arise?

1.68

- The leader is replaced by unscrupulous thugs.

  OR

- Crookedness diverts aristocratic leaders from their course.

35. What does Scipio believe should be allotted to the authority of the aristocrats?

1.69

NOT regal supremacy

36. What two advantages does Scipio think a mixed constitution has?

1.69

A widespread element of equality and stability.

37. In what ways does Scipio declare the Roman constitution to be superior?

1.70

Its structure, its assignment of functions, its discipline.

THE
REPUBLIC
Book 2

LESSON V: The Republic, Book 2.1-20

TEACHING NOTES

Homework Questions: 1, 2, 4, 5, 9, 10, 11, 15, 16, 19, 20, 21, 23, 24, 25, 26, 27, 28

Quiz Questions: 4, 15, 16, 19, 20, 24, 28

Discussion Focus Questions: 1

SYNOPSIS

Book 2.1-3 Preface: Comparison between Roman and Greek governments

4-20 Romulus

> 4 Birth and Childhood
>
> 4-9 Choosing the site
>
> 10-11 Founding Rome
>
> 12-13 The Sabines and Titus Tatius
>
> 14-16 Establishing the senate and auspices
>
> 17-20 Apotheosis

I. THOUGHT QUESTIONS:

1. Cicero acknowledges skeptical views of the apotheosis of Romulus, but asserts that the legend is valuable regardless of literal truth. Do you believe that accepting the legends of a nation's founders is important independent of their truthfulness? Why or why not?

   Teacher Note: If students have trouble with this, offer the example that George Washington almost certainly did not chop down a cherry tree, but the story is important because it communicates the value of truthfulness. Should we continue to tell it?

II. COMPREHENSION QUESTIONS:

1. What personal qualities does Scipio admire about Cato?

   2.1
   - temperate way of speaking
   - combination of seriousness and humor
   - zest for providing and obtaining information
   - close correspondence between his preaching and his practice

   Note: *Discuss to which Roman values each corresponds.*

2. Why did Cato believe the Roman constitution superior to others?

   2.2

   It had been made by many men over many generations.

3. Cato used to say that "no genius of such magnitude had ever existed that _____

   he could be sure of overlooking nothing (2.2) _____."

4. How is Cicero (through Scipio) breaking from the tradition of Socrates and Plato?

   2.3

   By describing the development of a real state rather than an imaginary community

5. On what grounds does Scipio ask his skeptic audience to accept Romulus's divine parentage?

   2.4

   The tradition was popular, and it was handed down by the forefathers.

6. Why did the country people readily accept the leadership of Romulus?

   2.4

   Because he was so far ahead of the others in physical strength and force of character.

7. According to Scipio, what tactical disadvantage does founding a city on the coast present?

   2.5

   Coastal cities are exposed to numerous and unforeseeable dangers.

8. According to Scipio, what tactical advantage does founding a city inland present?

   2.6

   You can see and hear enemies coming.

9. According to Scipio, with what moral disadvantages are coastal cities beset?

2.7-2.8

They are prone to corruption and decay because with so many foreigners, their ancestral institutions change, imported goods entice the people to luxury, and the beauty of the coast entices the people to idleness.

10. What does Scipio identify as "clearly" the cause of Greece's misfortunes?

2.9

Seafaring

11. What advantage does Scipio concede to coastal cities?

2.9

They are convenient for trade.

12. What are Rome's natural defenses?

2.11

Steep, precipituous mountains; a rampart and ditch; abundance of spring water.

13. With whom did Romulus share kingship, and why?

2.13

The outcome of the battle with the Sabines was uncertain, so Romulus made a treaty with them, in which he and Titus Tatius, the Sabine king, would be his partner in kingship and the Sabines would become Roman citizens.

14. Who established the "Fathers"?

2.14

Romulus and Titus Tatius

15. What are the Fathers?

2.14

A royal council made up of leading citizens.

16. What other political institutions did Romulus and Tatius establish?

2.14

They divided the populace into three tribes and into thirty voting districts.

17. What changed after Tatius's death?

2.14

Romulus relied more on the Fathers.

18. According to Scipio, when do monarchies function best?

2.15

When the influence of the best men is allowed to act upon the absolute monarch.

19. Who received the plunder from Romulus's wars?

2.15

Only the citizens, not Romulus himself.

20. What act marked the beginning of the Roman state?

2.16

Romulus taking auspices before founding the city.

21. What did Romulus do at the beginning of every public event?

2.16

One augur from each tribe assisted him in taking the auspices.

22. What was the origin of the patron-client system?

2.16

Romulus assigned the common people to leading citizens.

23. What were the first legal punishments established in Rome?

2.16

Fines of sheep and cattle rather than violent punishments.

24. What form did early Roman wealth take?

2.16

Livestock and land

25. What two "foundation-stones of the state" were established by Romulus?

2.17

The auspices and the Senate

Note: *Cicero was both a senator and an augur.*

26. How did Romulus "die"?

2.17

He failed to reappear after an eclipse of the sun, and is supposed to have been taken
into the company of the gods.

27. On what grounds does Scipio ask his skeptical audience to accept this tale of apotheosis?

2.18-2.19 – The less educated believe in myths, but at the time of Romulus, men
were civilized and educated, so this could not be mere mythic fabrication.

Note: *terrible argument*

28. Who is Quirinus?

2.20

The deified Romulus

LESSON VI: The Republic, Book 2.21-36

TEACHING NOTES

Homework Questions: 1, 2, 4, 5, 7, 9, 10, 11, 15, 17, 18, 19, 23, 24, 25

Quiz Questions: 1, 4, 7, 10, 11, 19

Discussion Focus Questions: 1

SYNOPSIS

Book 2.21-52 Early Kings

21-22 Plato, the Peripatetics, and Scipio

23-30 Numa

    23-24 Interregnum

    25 Election

    26-7 Numa's reign

    28-30 Numa and Pythagoras

31-32 Tullus Hostilius

33 Ancus Marcus

34-36 Tarquinius Priscus and the importation of Greek learning

I. THOUGHT QUESTIONS:

1. Cicero praises Rome's early kings for giving land and goods to the people, but criticizes the same acts in later politicians, calling it a symptom of populist tyranny. What do you think is the reason for this apparent inconsistency?

II. COMPREHENSION QUESTIONS:

1. What are Patricians?

    2.23

    The children of the Fathers

2. Why did the Senate not rule Rome by itself after the death of Romulus?

    2.23

    The people called out for a king.

3. What are the advantages of an interregnum?

    2.23

    The state is not without a monarch pending the election of a king, and he is not a long-reigning substitute.

4. What did the early Romans look for in a king?

    2.24

    Valor and good sense rather than noble lineage.

5. What was distinct about the origins of Numa Pompilius?

    2.25

    He was a Sabine from Cures, and was not living in Rome when he was elected.

6. How did Numa divert the Romans from military pursuits?

    2.26

    - He divided the territory among the citizens.
    - He encouraged them to work the land.
    - He instilled a love of peace and relaxation.

7. What things provide the most favorable conditions for the growth of justice and good faith?

    2.26

    Peace and relaxation

8. Describe Numa's religious reforms.

2.26-2.27

- He extended the scope of the auspices.
- He added 2 augurs.
- He appointed 5 priests.
- He created flamens.
- He created Salii.
- He created vestal virgins.
- He devised many rituals to be complex but inexpensive.

9. Why did Numa want to turn the Romans' attention to religious ceremonies?

2.26

To temper those ardent spirits which were accustomed to and eager for continual warfare.

10. How did Numa win the fierce and brutal Romans over to civilized behavior?

2.27

He instituted fairs, games, and other public gatherings.

11. According to Scipio, what two factors ensure that states will last?

2.27

Religion and humane behavior

12. Why is it not possible for Numa to have been a Pythagorean?

2.28-2.29

Pythagoras lived many years after Numa's death.

13. Why is Manilius happy that Numa was not a Pythagorean?

2.29

It means that Rome's culture is homegrown rather than imported from Greece.

14. According to Scipio, how did the Roman people become strong?

2.30

They became strong not by chance, although fortune was not against them, but through their own good sense and their firm system of values.

15. How did Tullus Hostilius become king?

2.31

He was declared king at a meeting of the Assembly of Voting Districts chaired by the interrex. His position as king was also ratified by each district in turn.

16. From where did the Senate house and the place for the people's assembly come?

2.31

Tullus Hostilius built them with the money from his war plunder.

17. What procedure did Tullus Hostilius formulate?

2.31

The legal procedure for declaring war.

18. According to Scipio, what deems a war unjust and unholy?

2.31

One that has not been declared and proclaimed.

19. What important point did the early kings of Rome grasp?

2.31

Certain rights should be granted to the people.

20. What were the major achievements of Ancus Marcius's kingship?

2.33

• He defeated the Latins and gave them citizenship.

• He extended the city to include the Aventine and Caelian hills.

• He distributed the conquered territory among the people.

• He established a colony and city at the mouth of the Tiber.

21. What was the "first step forward" in learning and culture for the Romans?

2.34

An influx of moral and artistic teaching from Greece.

22. How did Lucius Tarquinius become king?

2.35

He was a close friend of Ancus, and he possessed charm and kindness. He gave
help, assistance, protection, and financial aid to every citizen who needed it. Upon
Ancus's death, he was unanimously voted on as king.

23. How did Lucius Tarquinius reform the Senate?

2.35

He doubled their number, dividing them into "greater" and "lesser" families.

24. How did Lucius Tarquinius reform the equites?

2.36

He reorganized them and doubled their number, so there were 1,200 in all.

25. How did his reforms of the equites help Lucius Tarquinius?

2.36

He was able to defeat the Aequi in battle and drive off the Sabines from the city walls.

LESSON VII: The Republic, Book 2.37-70

TEACHING NOTES

Homework Questions: 3, 4, 5, 7, 8, 17, 18, 21, 22, 23, 24, 25, 27, 30, 31

Quiz Questions: 3, 4, 5, 7, 8, 21, 22, 31

Discussion Focus Questions: 1

SYNOPSIS

Book 2.37-43 Servius Tullius

    37-38 Transition and assumption of power

    39-40 Constitutional changes

    42-43 Decline of the monarchy

  44-52 Tarquinius Superbus

    44-52 Tyranny

    44-46 Revolution

    47-52 The despot vs. the statesman

53-70 Early Republic, Decemvirs

  53-60 Senate, consuls, the tribunate

    53-61 Aristocracy in the early republic

    53-56 Consulship

    57-60 The tribunate

  61-70 Decemvirs

    61-63 The oligarchic experiment of the decemvirate

    64-70 Analogies and conclusion

I. THOUGHT QUESTIONS:

1. In 2.39-2.45, Cicero asserts that the wealthy are most fit to rule, and the influence of the poor should be limited (that is, he advocates plutocracy). He does not, however, provide any evidence or justification, but assumes his readers' agreement. Whether or not you agree, come up with reasons both for and against this system.

II. COMPREHENSION QUESTIONS:

1. How did the son of a slave become king?

2.37

Servius Tullius waited at the king's table. His intelligence was so apparent that Lucius Tarquinius treated him as his son and had him thoroughly educated.

2. Why does Scipio say Servius Tullius was not formally chosen by the people even though he was acclaimed and ratified by the Assembly?

2.38

He was ruling in practice before he ruled in name and he did not submit himself to the Senate.

3. How did Servius Tullius rearrange the Assemblies to take power away from the people?

2.39

He organized them into five classes, and distributed them in such a way that most votes were in the hands of the wealthy.

4. Who are the assidui?

2.40

The rich

5. Who are the proletarii?

2.40

The poor

6. According to Scipio, why is a monarchy most liable to change, even with a senate?

2.43

"... when it is upset by the incompetence of one man, there is nothing to stop it from falling headlong into utter ruin."

7. How does Scipio define freedom?

2.43

Scipio defines freedom as having no master at all, even a just one.

8. Why did the people initially put up with Tarquinius Superbus even though he was harsh and unjust?

2.44

His military success brought wealth into Rome.

9. According to Scipio, what is the crowning achievement of political wisdom?

2.45

To divine the course of affairs so that you can hold them back or be ready to meet them.

10. According to Scipio, why was Tarquinius Superbus determined to terrify others?

2.45

He had the blood of a good king on his hands, and so he was terrified of paying the ultimate penalty for his crime.

11. When it comes to preserving the people's freedom, __no one is just a private citizen (2.46)__ .

12. What is the foulest and most repellent creature imaginable, the most abhorrent to gods and men alike?

2.48

A tyrant

13. According to Scipio, why can a tyrant not be properly called a man?

2.48

He "renounces every legal tie, every civilized partnership with his own citizens, and indeed with the entire human species."

14. According to Scipio, what sort of man can preserve the country?

2.51

The sort of man who can preserve the country is one who thoroughly understands what enhances the interests and prestige of the state, who is a guardian and overseer of his country.

15. Plato constructed a state which was __desirable__ rather than __feasible__ (2.52).

16. Why did Publius Valerius move his house?

2.53

The people resented that he had been building his house on the site where King Tullus had lived.

17. How did Publius Valerius show himself to be the people's friend?

2.53

He had enacted a law that no Roman citizen could be flogged or put to death without permitting an appeal.

> Note: *St. Paul, as a Roman citizen, appeals to this law in Acts 25, but the appeal is made to Caesar at that point in time, rather than to the assembly.*

18. How were most things done in the early republic?

2.56

On the authority of the Senate rather than the people.

19. Describe consular power in the early republic.

2.56

Consuls ruled only for one year, but otherwise were equivalent to kings.

20. What rule was vital in maintaining the power of the aristocracy?

2.56

The decisions of the Assemblies were not valid unless endorsed by the Senate's authority.

21. To preserve a government from change, the magistrates must have ___adequate power___, the aristocratic council ___adequate influence___, and the people ___adequate freedom___ (2.57).

22. How did the people originally get tribunes elected?

2.58-2.59

Through seditious (rebellious) action.

23. Why does Scipio dislike tribunes?

2.59

Because they reduce the power and authority of the Senate.

> Note: *Cicero was very opposed to Caesar, who used tribunician power to enact much legislation.*

24. Why was the authority of the Senate respected?

2.59

They enjoyed fewer pleasures than others and were not richer. They helped individual citizens by their actions, advice, and financial support.

25. What were the powers of the decemviri?

2.61

- supreme power not subject to appeal
- the drafting of laws

26. How often were the decemviri replaced?

2.61 – Annually

27. Why did Gaius Julius win great approval?

2.61

He only fined Lucius Sestius for an obvious murder, because he would not violate the law that only the Assembly could issue a death sentence.

28. Why could the system of the decemvirate not last long?

2.62

It could not last long because it was not equally just to all ranks of society.

29. Give an example of the injustice of the two extra law tables.

2.63

Prohibition against intermarriage between classes.

30. Why did the Romans discard the decemvirate and return to the former system of government?

2.63

The decemviri were corrupt and cruel, and there were no limits on their power.

31. To what does Scipio compare reason?

2.67

A man who controls an elephant while riding it.

32. Describe Scipio's ideal statesman.

2.69

He should have no other duties. He should never cease inspecting and examining himself, challenging others to imitate him, and offering himself as a mirror to his fellow citizens.

33. According to Scipio, what does concord in a state require?

2.69

Justice

THE REPUBLIC

Book 3

LESSON VIII: The Republic, Book 3.1-28

TEACHING NOTES

Homework Questions: 1, 5, 8, 9, 10, 11, 13, 15, 17, 18, 19, 26

Quiz Questions: 5, 8, 10, 11, 15, 19

Discussion Focus Questions: 1, 2

SYNOPSIS

Book 3.1-28 The Folly of Justice

1-7 Preface

8-28 Philus argues against justice

8-13 Summaries

13-18 Legal inconsistency

18-25 Justice as utility

26-28 Human failure and conclusion

I. THOUGHT QUESTIONS:

1. Philus asserts that justice is political rather than natural, and Laelius argues that justice is a function of natural (and universal) law. Which do you think is more likely, and why? Be sure to refute the arguments of the other side.

2. Much of Book 3 discusses the relationship between legality and justice. What do you perceive this relationship to be?

3. Come up with at least one example for and against Carneades' argument.

4. Teacher Note: Carneades' argument relies on an implicit assumption that there is constant competition for resources. His argument is somewhat plausible to the point required for survival, but beyond that necessitates human greed.

II. COMPREHENSION QUESTIONS:

1. What does Cicero assert brought together people who had previously lived apart?

   3.3

   The delightful bond of a common speech.

   Note: *This makes very little sense. A common speech is much likelier to develop out of proximity than the other way around.*

2. According to Cicero, what is uniquely changeless and eternal?

   3.3

   Numbers

3. According to Cicero, what produces an almost incredible and superhuman kind of excellence?

   3.4

   The art of governing and training people.

4. According to Cicero, whom should everyone acknowledge is superior to everyone else?

   3.5

   One who adds scholarship and deeper understanding to his native intelligence and what he knows of the state.

   Note: *He is talking about himself here.*

5. If forced to choose between scholarship and statecraft, which course does Cicero recommend?

   3.6

   Statecraft

6. According to Cicero, what is required to devise a form of government that will last?

   3.7

   Practical wisdom of the very highest order.

7. What does Philus call "a splendid case"?

   3.8

   The defense of wickedness.

8. According the Philus, what is the simplest way of getting at the truth?

   3.8

   Arguing both sides of a case.

9. According the Philus, what virtue is most generous and open-handed and loves everyone better than itself?

   3.12

   Justice

10. What does Philus contend is the weakness of Plato and Aristotle in advocating justice?

3.13

Justice is a political phenomenon, not an element in nature.

11. If justice were part of nature, it would be _____the same_____ for _____everyone_____ (3.13).

12. What example does Philus give of Roman injustice against the Gauls?

3.16

They are forbidden to plant olive trees and vines in order to enhance the value of Roman products.

13. Philus holds this policy up as an example that _____wisdom_____ is different from _____fairness_____ (3.16).

14. What is the point of Philus's discussion of the changes in womens' legal rights in Rome?

3.17

To undermine the idea that law and justice are related or natural.

15. According to Philus, how would things be different if justice were a function of nature?

3.18

Every country would have the same laws, and one country would not have different laws at different times.

16. According the Philus, naturally good men abide by _____real_____, not merely _____putative_____ (3.18), justice.

17. How does Philus's Roman example support his argument that some laws are not just, but expedient?

3.19

Killing is not lawful or just under normal circumstances, but it is at times expedient, and so there is a procedure by which it can be made legal, though it remains unjust.

18. Summarize Carneades' argument that there is no natural law.

3.19

Humans seek what is in their own interests. Acting in another's interest deprives oneself (presumably of property).

19. According to Philus, what causes the compromise of mixed government?

3.23

Mutual fear between classes and individuals.

20. According to Philus, what is the mother of justice?

3.23

Weakness, rather than nature or good intentions.

21. According to Philus, what does wisdom encourage us to do?

3.24

Wisdom encourages us to make money, increase our possessions, extend our boundaries, rule over as many subjects as possible, enjoy pleasures, and revel in power, supremacy, and dominion.

22. According to Philus, what does justice teach?

3.24

Justice teaches "to spare all men, take thought for the interests of mankind, give everyone his due, and not lay hands on the things belonging to the gods, the state, or somebody else."

23. According to Philus, why do the Epicureans have more weight in argument than others?

3.26

When discussing the good man, they do not argue "like cunning old hands full of evil intent."

24. Describe the Epicurean good man.

3.26

He lives a life free from fear, worry, anxiety, and danger because he is good and just.

25. Describe the Epicurean wicked man.

3.26

He is full of qualms and fears, and his profits and rewards fail to make up for his dread of punishment.

26. Through the example of Pompeius and Mancinus, what virtues does Philus associate with politically disadvantageous justice and which with politically advantageous injustice?

3.28

- **disadvantageous justice:** self-respect, integrity, honor
- **advantageous injustice:** clear-headedness, practical common sense, awareness of the state's real interests

LESSON IX: The Republic, Book 3.29-48

TEACHING NOTES

Homework Questions: 2, 3, 6, 7, 8, 9, 13, 14, 15

Quiz Questions: 6, 7, 8, 9, 5

Discussion Focus Questions: 1 or 2, 3

SYNOPSIS

Book 3.29-46 Natural Law

    32-41 Laelius argues for justice

        32-39 Natural morality

        40-43 Immortality of the soul and the rewards of virtue

        34-41 Injustice is fatal to a state

        42-48 Justice in government

I. THOUGHT QUESTIONS:

1. Consider the conflict between Agamemnon and Achilles. Argue for each how he was right, just and wise.

2. Consider the trial of Orestes in Aeschylus' Oresteia. Outline a short defense and prosecution of Orestes. Be sure to consider the rightness, justice, and wisdom of his actions and their interaction with the law.

3. Come up with examples and support for Laelius's assertions about natural law in 3.33, and refute Laelius's assertions about natural law in 3.33.

II. COMPREHENSION QUESTIONS:

1. Why does Laelius think Carneades should not be allowed to address Rome's youth?

   3.32

   His remarks are outrageous, and if he believes them, he is a filthy scoundrel.

   Note: Id est, they are inconsistent with Roman values.

2. According to Laelius, what is law in the proper sense?

   3.33

   Right reason in harmony with nature.

3. What examples and support does Laelius provide for his assertion that natural law is unchanging, eternal, and universal?

   3.33

   There is a single divine law, and it is the nature of humans to obey it.

   Note: This religiously based argument is an interesting choice for a skeptic and follower of Plato. It also is a further assertion, rather than support, per se.

4. According to Laelius, how should a state be organized?

   3.34

   In such a way as to last forever.

5. What is the death of a state?

   3.34

   Unnatural; it is as if the whole world were to collapse and pass away.

6. What makes a war just or unjust?

   3.35

   A war is unjust if it is undertaken without proper cause; for any reason other than repelling an enemy or for punishing an enemy; it must be declared and proclaimed; redress (presumably non-violent) must have been previously sought.

7. According to Laelius, over what does the mind rule like a king over subjects?

   3.37

   The body

8. According to Laelius, over what does the mind rule like a master crushing the spirits of his slaves?

   3.37

   Desire and anger

9. Why does a good man not seek incentives such as power and kingdoms?

3.40

Because they are human possessions and he regards his own goods as divine.

10. If goodness is deprived of rewards, how does it sustain itself?

3.40

With its own beauty.

11. On what grounds does Laelius deny the Apotheosis of Hercules and Romulus?

3.40

"… nature would not allow that something with an earthly origin should exist anywhere except on earth."

12. According to Laelius, what was the error of Tiberius Gracchus?

3.41

He acted properly toward Roman citizens, but ignored the rights of the Latin allies which were guaranteed by treaty.

13. According to Laelius, what is the outcome of such lawless behavior?

3.41

Justice becomes violence, and those who formerly accepted Rome's authority willingly will be loyal only out of fear, which could eventually cause the downfall of the empire.

14. Why does Scipio refuse to call Syracuse a republic?

3.43

It is ruled by one man, and a republic is the property of the public.

15. Why does Laelius refuse to call a republic a state which is totally controlled by the masses?

3.45 – There is no "public" except when it is held together by a legal agreement, so a mob can be just as tyrannical as a single despot.

Note: *This is true (sometimes called the tyranny of the majority), however, he clearly makes no distinction between a mob (which lacks formal process and deliberation) and a democracy (in which there is formal process and deliberation). Social climber that Cicero was, it probably never occurred to him that we hoi polloi have the capacity for rational political thought.*

16. According to Mummius, what kind of state is the most fortunate, and what kind is most defective?

3.46

The most fortunate state is one in which several good men are in charge of affairs; the most defective is one with unfettered democracy.

17. Describe the government of Rhodes.

3.48

All citizens were both common people and senators. A rota system decided when they were each. They received payment for governing in both capacities. The senate had as much power and prestige as the masses.

THE REPUBLIC

Books 4 & 5

LESSON X: The Republic, Books 4 and 5

Begin reading at Section 10.

TEACHING NOTES

Homework Questions: 3, 4, 5, 6, 9, 10, 11, 18, 19

Quiz Questions: 4, 5, 6, 11, 19

Discussion Focus Questions: 1

SYNOPSIS

BOOKS 4 & 5: Shame, Corruption, and the Mos Maiorum

Book 4: Roman social institutions

    3-4 Youth

    4-5 Plato

    6 Women, censorship

    8 Law in society

    9-14 Theater

Book 5: The Statesman

    1-2 Moral institutions

    3-11 The statesman

    3 Lawgiver

    4-5 Understanding

    6-8 Moral compass

    9-11 Virtues

I. THOUGHT QUESTIONS:

1. What does Scipio's speech on corruption in 5.11 indicate about the relationship between law and justice? **Note:** Begin with the implication that a legal ruling and a legal vote can still be, according to Scipio, corrupt.

II. COMPREHENSION QUESTIONS: *Begin reading at Section 10.*

1. How did the ancient Romans regard the theater?

   4.10

   Disgraceful; They denied public office and suffrage to those who associated with it.

2. What evidence does Cicero present that vices were condoned in everyday life?

   4.11

   The audiences approved of them in comedies.

3. According to Cicero, who has the right to criticize a citizen's lifestyle?

   4.12 – The law and the magistrates rather than poets.

   Note: *Cicero took himself far more seriously than did the poets of his day. Worse yet, he could not respond in kind, because he was an abysmal poet. He was, however, a brilliant orator, hence his insistence that the only proper arena for criticism is the courts.*

4. According to Cicero, what two things are necessary for founding and maintaining a great empire?

   5.1

   Old-fashioned men and ancient customs (from the poet Ennius)

5. According to Cicero, how did his generation treat the mos maiorum?

   5.2

   Cicero's generation treated it like a magnificent picture which it refused to restore, and neglected until the original could hardly be seen.

6. According to Cicero, why had Rome lost the name and substance of Republic?

   5.2

   Moral failings

7. According to Manilius, why should kings have property set aside for them and land worked on their behalf?

   5.3 – So they would not be distracted from public concerns by any worries over their private business.

   Note: *While this does make sense, it does not explain why kings tend to have so very much more property and wealth than they need.*

8. To whom does Manilius attribute this form of kingship?

   5.3

   The Greeks

9. Why does Manilius approve of Numa's kingship particularly?

5.3

Because he was undistracted by war and was able to focus on law and religion.

10. According to Scipio, why must a statesman avoid answering queries, reading cases, and writing decisions?

5.5

Because he must be free to manage and keep account of the state.

11. According to Scipio, in what two aspects of law does a statesman need to be versed?

5.5

The fundamental principles; civil law

12. According to Scipio, why do the best men avoid breaking the law?

5.6

To avoid shame.

13. How does Scipio define shame?

5.6

That dread of justified rebuke which nature has imparted to man.

14. How does a statesman develop a sense of shame?

5.6

Public opinion, education, social training.

15. According to Scipio, what is required for a good life?

5.7

A good state

16. According to Scipio, what is the greatest blessing?

5.7

A well-ordered state

17. According to Scipio, what is the greatest task any man can have?

5.8

The greatest task any man can have is the task of the statesman, that is, ensuring the citizens a life secure in wealth, rich in resources, abundant in renown, and honorable in its moral character.

18. In what ways does Scipio assert a vote or a verdict can be corrupted?

5.11

By money and by eloquence.

19. "No honest man can be corrupted by _____ a bribe _____ , but he *can* be corrupted by _____ eloquence (5.11) _____."

THE REPUBLIC

Book 6

LESSON XI: The Republic, Book 6

TEACHING NOTES

Homework Questions: 5, 7, 9, 10, 11, 13, 14, 19, 20, 22, 23, 24, 28, 32, 33, 36, 37, 38, 39, 40, 42

Quiz Questions: 7, 19, 20, 24, 36, 38, 39, 40

Discussion Focus Questions: 1

SYNOPSIS

Book 6: The Dream of Scipio

        8 Rewards of the statesman

        3-6 Contrast with Plato and the myth of Er

        9-10 Masinissa

        11-12 Scipio's death

        13-16 Afterlife

        17-19 Composition of the cosmos

        20-25 Glory and rewards

        26-28 Immortality of the soul

        29 Serving the commonwealth

I. THOUGHT QUESTIONS:

1. What do you think was Cicero's purpose in turning away from politics to a lengthy discussion of Platonic and Pythagorean cosmology? Does it change the way you, the reader, perceive his work?

II. COMPREHENSION QUESTIONS:

1. Why did King Masinissa weep and give thanks on Scipio's arrival?

   6.9

   In memory of his grandfather, Scipio Africanus.

2. To what rational origin does Scipio attribute his dream?

   6.10

   That he had been talking to Masinissa about his grandfather.

3. What did Africanus look like?

   6.10

   More like his portrait than he had in real life.

4. What was Scipio's reaction on seeing his grandfather?

   6.10

   He was afraid and trembled.

5. What did Africanus show to Scipio?

   6.11 – Carthage

6. According to Africanus, what would Scipio have to do in his 56th year?

   6.12

   Assume the dictatorship and restore order in the state.

   Note: He never did this. Perhaps Cicero wished he had. Cicero also asserts that Scipio was murdered by his family. He did die in the year in which Cicero set De Re Publica, but of natural causes.

7. According to Africanus, what happens to good statesmen when they die?

   6.13

   They have a place in heaven and enjoy a life of eternal bliss.

8. According to Africanus, what is most welcome to God?

   6.13 – states

9. According to Africanus, from where do rulers of states come?

   6.13 – from heaven

10. To what does Paulus compare the body?

    6.14 – a prison

11. What does Paulus call life?

    6.14 – death

12. What is the temple of the god Paulus describes?

6.15

The whole visible universe

13. According to Paulus, under what condition are humans born?

6.15

They must look after the earth.

14. According to Paulus, from where does the soul come?

6.15

It is given to humans out of those eternal fires known as stars and planets.

15. How does Paulus describe the planets?

6.15

They are round and spherical; they have divine minds; they complete their orbits with amazing speed.

16. According to Paulus, when can Scipio depart life?

6.15

Scipio can depart life when he receives the command of God.

17. Why must Scipio wait until that point?

6.15

Otherwise, he will be judged to have deserted the earthly post assigned to him by God.

18. What does Paulus tell Scipio to do?

6.16

Respect justice and do your duty.

19. According to Paulus, what way of life leads to heaven?

6.16

Respecting justice and doing your duty.

20. According to Paulus, where do souls (of good men) live when released from their bodies?

6.16

The Milky Way

21. According to Paulus, how large are stars relative to the earth?

6.16

They easily exceed the earth in size.

22. How did Scipio respond to this shift in perspective?

6.16

It made him ashamed that the empire was so small.

23. Describe the spheres Africanus describes to Scipio.

6.17 – The outermost sphere is the heavens with the fixed stars. Inside that are the "wandering stars," i.e., planets, which move backward. The next sphere is Saturn, then Jupiter (who brings health and prosperity); then Mars (the dread red star); then the sun (which rules others, regulates the universe, and is so huge it fills everything with its light); then Venus and Mercury (attendants of the sun that follow it); then the moon (which is lit by the sun); then the earth (the lowest and heavy things fall on it).

Note on backward motion: *From the perspective of the earth, planets do indeed appear to move West to East while the stars appear to move East to West.* **Note on the planets:** *Cicero gets them in the correct order of distance from the earth.*

Note on the system: *Cicero is following the model of Archimedes, in which the sun is placed in the middle, rather than the model of Plato, in which the sun is between Venus and the moon. He is drawing a comparison between the sun and the statesman, so this is imperative.*

24. To what does Africanus compare the sun?

6.17

To the statesman.

Note: *This places the statesman at the center of the universe.*

25. According to Africanus, to what are all things below the moon subject?

6.17

Death and decay

26. According to Africanus, what are all things above the moon?

6.17

Eternal

27. Describe the music of the spheres.

> 6.18-6.19
>
> The momentum of the spheres produces sounds which are in harmony with one another. The outermost (heavenly) sphere produces the highest pitch because it is moving most quickly and therefore has the most frequent vibrations. The lowest sphere (the moon) makes the deepest note. The moon and the heavens are an octave apart, and it is from this harmony that human music is derived. The earth does not move, and so it makes no sound. Humans do not hear the music of the spheres because it is so loud that we have become deaf to it.
>
> **Note:** *Pythagorean in origin*

28. What does Africanus mean when he tells Scipio that people who stand at a different angle will not praise him?

> 6.20 – They are so far away that no matter how famous he becomes, they will not have heard of him.
>
> **Note:** *This makes sense only when you keep in mind that Cicero assumed the earth to be spherical.*

29. Describe the "belts" of the earth.

> 6.21
>
> There are five: The outermost are the poles and are frozen; the middle one is too hot for people to live; and the other two are habitable.

30. What is the point of Africanus's description of Europe?

> 6.22
>
> To point out to Scipio that his fame will never travel far.

31. According to Africanus, how long will the memory of Scipio and his family last to those who hear of them?

> 6.24 – Less than one year.
>
> **Note:** *The typical Greek (and somewhat) Roman idea of the afterlife was fairly bleak. The only chance of eternity or reward in the afterlife was dependent upon fame on earth. To be remembered was imperative.*

32. Describe "the great year."

> 6.24
>
> When all the heavenly bodies return to their original positions.
>
> **Note:** *12,954 years*

33. What portent does Africanus take to be the marker of "the great year"?

6.24

The same sort of solar eclipse that occurred with the death/apotheosis of Romulus.

Note: By starting the clock of cosmic time with this event, Cicero is establishing the importance of Rome to the cosmos. He has already established that the statesman is to the state what the sun is to the universe (the center and ruler). For Cicero, the political events of Rome and his time are of eternal rather than temporal significance.

34. According to Africanus, how should Scipio NOT measure his destiny?

6.25

By the rewards of men.

35. What has Scipio done since boyhood?

6.26

Followed in the footsteps of Africanus and Paulus.

36. According to Africanus, what is a man's "true self"?

6.26

His mind

37. Why does Africanus say that Scipio is a god?

6.26

He rules over his body just as God rules over the universe.

38. According to Africanus, what is mortal and what is immortal?

6.26

The soul and God are immortal.

The body and the universe are mortal.

Note: The soul or mind alone as eternal is platonic.

39. According to Africanus, what causes death?

6.27

The cessation of motion

Note: All of section 6.27 is a direct quote from Plato.

40. On what grounds does Africanus assert that the mind is eternal?

6.28

It moves itself.

41. According to Africanus, what are the best concerns?

6.29

Concerns for the safety of one's country.

42. According to Africanus, what speeds the soul toward heaven?

6.29

Concern for the state, contemplation of what lies beyond death.

43. According to Africanus, what happens after death to the souls of men who seek pleasure?

6.29

They are buffeted about on earth for many ages.

Note: *Cicero begins and ends the Republic with a criticism of Epicureans.*

THE
LAWS

THE LAWS SYNOPSIS

BOOK 1

1-16 Introductions

> 1-5 Types of truth

> 5-10 Persuading Cicero to write history

> 10-16 Laws for the ideal republic

17-35 Natural Law

> 17-18 Natural and civil law

> 18-20 Law in nature, right reason

> 21-27 Reason shared between gods and men

> 28-35 Reason is universal

36-57 Justice and Virtue

> 36-39 Peripatetic ideas of the good

> 40-42 Justice is separate from human law and human limitations

> 42-46 Nature as the universal standard of justice

> 47 Human failings obscure virtue

> 48-52 Justice as its own end

52-57 Disputes over semantics

58-63 Conclusion and commentary on philosophy

BOOK 2

1-22 Cicero's Religious Law Code

> 1-7 Double citizenship

> 8-14 Natural law and civil law

> 14-18 Introduction to the law

> 19-22 Cicero's ideal law code: religious laws

>> 19 Which gods should be worshiped

>> 19-20 Ritual calendar

>> 20-21 Priesthoods

>> 21-22 Religious prohibitions, obligations to the deceased, funerals

23-69 Commentary on Cicero's Religious Law Code

> 23-68 Commentary on Cicero's ideal religious laws

>> 23-24 Introduction

>> 24-28 Worship

>> 29 Ritual calendar

>> 29-34 Priesthoods

>> 35-45 Religious prohibitions

>> 45-68 Obligations to the deceased and funeral regulations

> 69 Conclusion

BOOK 3

THE
LAWS
Book 1

LESSON XII: The Laws, Book 1.1-35

TEACHING NOTES

Homework Questions: Memorize participants in the dialogue, 2, 3, 14, 16, 17, 19, 23, 24, 25, 28, 30, 32, 33, 34, 40, 41, 42, 43, 47, 49, 53, 55, 56, 58, 59, 60, 62

Quiz Questions: participants in the dialogue, 2, 3, 16, 25, 30, 32, 47, 49, 53, 55, 56, 58, 60

SYNOPSIS

Book 1.1-35 Natural Law

1-16 Introductions

    1-5 Types of truth

    5-10 Persuading Cicero to write history

    10-16 Laws for the ideal republic

17-35 Natural Law

    17-18 Natural and civil law

    18-20 Law in nature, right reason

    21-27 Reason shared between gods and men

    28-35 Reason is universal

I. THOUGHT QUESTIONS:

1. Cicero asserts that justice is a function of nature evident in all human societies. Write an argument that this is the case, and an argument that this isn't the case. Do not recycle Cicero's reasons.

II. PARTICIPANTS IN THE DIALOGUE:

Marcus: Marcus Tullius Cicero, our esteemed author

Quintus: Quintus Tullius Cicero. Our author's younger brother. In the year in which the dialogue is set, he was actually a legate for Caesar in Gaul. He supported Caesar in the civil wars and tried to dissuade his brother from his steadfast support of Pompey. They were both killed in proscriptions after Caesar's death.

Atticus: Titus Pomponius Atticus, Cicero's lifelong friend, and Quintus's brother in law. He lived in Athens (hence his cognomen). Cicero wrote hundreds of letters to him. As an Epicurean, he stayed out of public life. He had a reputation for being able to get along with everyone, no matter the difficult circumstances.

III. COMPREHENSION QUESTIONS:

1. How do things survive longer than they can naturally last?

   1.2

   By virtue of tradition.

2. Why does Cicero inquire about the legends of Quirinus and Orithyia?

   1.4

   Cicero inquires to make a point about respecting mythological tradition for its own sake rather than examining it for literal truth.

3. What two kinds of truth does Cicero explain?

   1.5

   Historical truth and poetic truth (which is meant to entertain).

4. In what field does Atticus believe Roman literature to be lacking?

   1.5

   History

5. Why does Atticus think Cicero should be the one to fill this need?

   1.5 – Atticus says he thinks Marcus owes it as a duty to his country, and it is closely akin to oratory.

6. List Atticus's criticisms of Roman historians.

   1.6-1.7

   Fabius, Cato, Piso, Fannius, Vennonius - insipid

   Coelius Antipater - lacks polish and finesse

   Gellius, Clodius, Asellio - slack and incompetent

   Macer - poor rhetoric and lacks propriety

   Sisenna - childish and mediocre

7. About what does Atticus want Cicero to write?

   1.8

   The events to which he was witness, i.e., the achievements of Pompey and his own consulship.

8. Why doesn't Cicero want to write a history?

   1.8-1.9

   He doesn't have enough uninterrupted time.

9. How does Cicero want to spend his old age?

1.10

Advising clients and writing (all while sitting in a chair).

10. How does Atticus think Cicero should spend his old age?

1.11

Continuing to speak in court and practicing oratory.

11. How does Quintus think Cicero should spend his old age?

1.12

Giving advice on the law.

12. What does Cicero believe is lacking in those before him who have expounded on civil law?

1.14

They have focused only on the details.

13. According to Cicero, what is practically necessary but intellectually undemanding?

1.14

Making civil law available to the people.

14. What aspect of law does Atticus want Cicero to discuss?

1.15

The laws of the ideal republic, i.e., a utopian legal code.

15. According to Cicero, what must be clarified before the source of law and justice can be identified?

1.16

The nature of man, the excellence of the human mind, the purpose and function of man, what unites people, what bonds people together in fellowship.

16. From what does Cicero believe law to be derived?

1.17

From philosophy rather than civil law or precedent.

17. According to Cicero, from what is the nature of justice deduced?

1.17

From the nature of man.

18. What topics does Cicero intend to discuss?

1.17

Universal law, ideal law, actual law.

19. According to Cicero, what is the highest reason inherent in nature?

1.18 – Law

Note: *This is a Stoic assertion.*

20. How does natural law function?

1.18

It enjoins what ought to be done and forbids the opposite.

21. What essential properties of law does Cicero derive from the etymologies of the Greek and Latin terms?

1.19

Fairness and choice

22. According to Cicero, from what must the origin of justice be derived?

1.19

Law

23. According to Cicero, what do learned men call law?

1.19

Law is a force of nature, the intelligence and reason of a wise man, and the criterion of justice and injustice.

Note: *He probably means the Stoics.*

24. According to Cicero, what does the man in the street call law?

1.19

Law is that which lays down in writing what it wishes to enjoin or forbid.

25. What does Cicero claim will guide his discussion of the origins of justice?

1.20 – Nature

26. What premise does Cicero ask Atticus to accept?

1.21

That nature is ruled by the immortal gods.

27. What is Cicero's definition of man?

1.22

A creature of foresight, wisdom, variety, keenness, memory, reason, and judgment.

28. According to Cicero, what separates man from the animals?

1.22 – Reason and reflection

Note: This is a Stoic view.

29. How does Cicero define wisdom?

1.22

Wisdom is the faculty of reason developed and become complete.

30. Summarize Cicero's argument that men are the partners of the gods in law.

1.23

Men and gods share reason.

Reason is the law.

Ergo men and gods share the law.

31. According to Cicero, what do those who share law share?

1.23

Justice

32. According to Cicero, how can the universe be considered a single community shared by gods and men?

1.23

Men and gods share justice in law, ergo they share the same state. Moreover, they are all subject to the same authority, an all-powerful god.

33. According to Cicero, where did humans come from?

1.24

They were scattered and sown in the earth, and given minds by God.

34. According to Cicero, why are humans of a common origin with the gods?

1.24

The mind was given by God.

35. According to Cicero, how do we know that mankind is of a common stock with the gods?

1.24

Only humans have a conception of God, and all humans believe in some kind of god.

36. According to Cicero, what does man recognize in God?

1.25

His place of origin

37. According to Cicero, what is moral excellence?

1.25

The completion and perfection of nature that is shared only by mankind and the gods.

38. According to Cicero, how does mankind acquire the necessities of life?

1.25-1.26

They are either given by nature or are acquired by reason copying nature.

39. According to Cicero, why did nature give man senses?

1.26-1.27

To act as servants and messengers.

40. According to Cicero, why did nature give man perceptions?

1.26-1.27

As the foundation of knowledge.

41. According to Cicero, why did nature give man a versatile physique?

1.26-1.27

So we can stand erect and contemplate the heavens.

42. According to Cicero, why did nature give man facial features?

1.26-1.27

To communicate emotional states and character.

43. According to Cicero, why did nature give man voice and speech?

1.26-1.27

They promote human fellowship.

44. According to Cicero, why did God create man in this way?

1.27

He intended man to take precedence over everything else.

45. According to Cicero, what strengthens and completes human reason?

1.27

Nature

46. According to Cicero, for what is mankind born?

1.28

Justice

47. To what does Cicero attribute individual differences between people?

1.29

We are naturally identical, but corrupt habits and foolish opinions twist and turn our feeble minds from their original paths.

Note: *This is a Platonic idea.*

48. According to Cicero, how can any member of any nation attain moral excellence?

1.30

By using nature as his guide.

49. What does Cicero believe about the nature of vice?

1.31

Pleasure leads to vice. Pleasure resembles what is naturally good, so through it vice can be mistakenly accepted as something beneficial.

50. According to Cicero, why is death shunned?

1.31

Because of the misconception that our true nature dies.

51. According to Cicero, why is life sought?

1.31

Because it preserves the condition in which we were born.

52. According to Cicero, why is pain considered evil?

1.31

Because it is harsh and seems to dissolve our nature.

53. According to Cicero, why are those who receive public honors considered blessed and the obscure pitied?

1.32

Because good character and good reputation look alike.

54. What does Cicero think of Egyptian religion?

1.32

He dismisses it as superstitious animal worship.

55. According to Cicero, what do all communities love?

1.32

Friendliness, generosity, appreciation for kindness.

56. According to Cicero, what do all communities reject and hate?

1.32

The arrogant, the wicked, the cruel, and the ungrateful.

57. According to Cicero, what makes everyone a better person?

1.32

The principles of right living

58. According to Cicero, how has nature given justice to mankind?

1.33

Nature has endowed us with reason, hence right reason, hence law, hence justice.

59. According to Cicero, does everyone have justice, or is it an attribute only of the wise?

1.33

Reason has been bestowed on everybody. Therefore, the same applies to justice because justice is an outgrowth of reason.

60. What did Socrates claim was the source of everything pernicious?

1.33

The separation of self-interest from justice.

61. According to Cicero, what is the product of showing goodwill to someone endowed with moral excellence?

1.34

That he loves the other person as much as he loves himself.

62. According to Cicero, what is the essential feature of friendship?

1.34

Putting the other person before oneself.

LESSON XIII: The Laws, Book 1.36-57

TEACHING NOTES

Homework Questions: 3, 4, 5, 6, 7, 9, 11, 12, 13, 18, 24, 25, 26, 27, 28, 32, 35, 36, 37, 38, 39, 40, 41, 44, 49

Quiz Questions: 9, 11, 12, 13, 27, 35, 36, 41, 44

Discussion Focus Questions: 1, 2, 4

SYNOPSIS

Book 1.36-57 Justice and Virtue

36-39 Peripatetic ideas of the good

40-42 Justice is separate from human law and human limitations

42-46 Nature as the universal standard of justice

47 Human failings of obscure virtue

48-52 Justice as its own end

52-57 Disputes over semantics

58-63 Conclusion and commentary on philosophy

I. THOUGHT QUESTIONS:

1. Cicero chooses to dismiss the Epicureans and the later Academy rather than refute their arguments or address their disagreements. Do you believe this weakens his case? Come up with two reasons why and two reasons why not.

2. Why do you think Cicero chooses to ignore disagreement rather than counter it?

3. Cicero asserts that justice is a function of nature evident in all human societies. Write an argument that this is the case, and an argument that this isn't the case. Do not recycle Cicero's reasons.

4. What advantage might a man get out of helping another man? Is that action still good? Does a self-serving motivation nullify the goodness of an action, or are actions good or bad independent of motivations? If a self-serving motivation nullifies the goodness, to what extent does it do so?

5. Do you agree with Cicero that things that are good are absolutely measurable independent of personal opinion? Come up with at least two examples both for and against this idea.

II. COMPREHENSION QUESTIONS:

1. What is the aim of Cicero's thesis?

   1.37

   His aim is to bring stability to states, steadiness to cities, and well-being to communities.

2. According to Cicero, what should not be regarded as a great good?

   1.37-1.38

   Anything that cannot truly be praised for its own sake.

3. Whom does Cicero believe his argument that justice is natural should satisfy?

   1.38

   The Old Academy, the Peripatetics, the Stoics

4. To whom does Cicero believe his argument is unsatisfactory?

   1.39

   The Epicureans and the New Academy

5. How does Cicero deal with their anticipated disagreement?

   1.39

   He dismisses rather than addresses it.

6. According to Cicero, when is no expiation possible?

   1.40

   When it comes to acts of wickedness against men and sacrilege against the gods.

7. According to Cicero, what happens to those offenders?

   1.40

   The Furies torment them with guilt.

8. What does Cicero believe about the courts?

   1.40

   They didn't always exist, don't exist everywhere, and aren't always sound.

9. According to Cicero, under what conditions does society lose the distinction between the just and the unjust?

   1.40

   When it is the fear of punishment that deters people from crime rather than distaste for wickedness.

10. According to Cicero, what sort of people are good for the sake of advantage rather than for the sake of goodness?

  1.41 – The crafty rather than the good.

  > **Note:** *He's talking about the Epicureans. He really does dismiss them without making any attempt to understand their doctrines beyond the most superficial aspects.*

11. According to Cicero, how would a good man and an advantage-seeking man act toward a helpless rich stranger met on the road?

  1.41

  The good man helps him, and the advantage-seeking man either kills him and robs him, or refrains from it only because he is afraid of being found out and punished.

12. According to Cicero, what is most foolish of all?

  1.42

  The belief that everything decreed by institutions or laws of a particular country is just.

13. What is Cicero's justification for saying some laws of nations are unjust?

  1.42

  They are opposed to natural justice and natural law.

14. According to Cicero, who is unjust?

  1.42

  The man who does not acknowledge the law of right reason.

15. According to Cicero, what destroys the justice that only serves self-interest?

  1.42-1.43

  Self-interest

16. According to Cicero, from where do the virtues of liberality, patriotism, and devotion arise?

  1.43

  These virtues are rooted in the fact that we are inclined by nature to have a regard for others, which is the basis of justice.

17. According to Cicero, why should man practice religion?

  1.43

  Not out of fear, but out of the association between man and God.

18. To show that justice is not a matter of mere legality, what examples does Cicero give of unjust things that could be made legal?

1.43

Robbery, adultery, forging wills

19. According to Cicero, what must every praiseworthy good have?

1.46

It must have within itself something to be praised.

20. According to Cicero, what determines goodness?

1.46

Nature rather than people's opinions.

21. According to Cicero, what is the cause of the belief that some ideas are illusory?

1.47

When they vary from person to person, and do not remain consistent within the same person.

22. How does Cicero account for this inconsistency?

1.47

People and pleasure lay traps for our minds. Pleasure makes us unable to see clearly what is naturally good, because it is not as exciting as pleasure.

23. According to Cicero, what is the mother of all ills?

1.47

Pleasure

24. According to Cicero, what do all good men love?

1.48

What is fair in itself and what is right in itself.

25. According to Cicero, is generosity for free or for profit?

1.48

When a person is open-handed without reward, it's free. When he looks for profit, it is investment.

26. According to Cicero, what is the cause and meaning of all the virtues?

1.48

Justice

27. According to Cicero, what is goodness sought for its own advantages?

1.49

Selfishness

28. According to Cicero, what things should be cherished for their own sake?

1.49

Friendship, human fellowship, fairness, justice

29. According to Cicero, what is the worst kind of injustice?

1.49

To look for profit from justice.

30. According to Cicero, from what can one infer a soul's ugliness?

1.51

From its vices.

31. According to Cicero, how is goodness most convincingly revealed?

1.52

In scorning and rejecting pleasure.

32. According to Cicero, what is the standard and goal of every action?

1.52

The ultimate good

33. What did Gellius call the controversies of the Philosophers?

1.53

Futile squabbles

34. According to Cicero, what is the only relevant disagreement between the Old Academy and Zeno?

1.54

The Academy held that everything in conformity with nature that helped us in life was good, whereas Zeno thought that nothing was good unless it was honorable.

Note: *This is an extreme simplification that Cicero takes from Antiochus.*

35. According to Cicero, what does Zeno call the only good?

1.55-1.56

What is honorable.

36. How does this differ from the Old Academy?

1.55

It allowed for other goods, believing what is honorable only to be the highest.

37. According to Cicero, what does Zeno call the only evil? _____ 1.55 – Disgrace

38. How is this different from the Old Academy?

1.55

They allow for other evils, believing disgrace to be the worst.

39. According to Cicero, what does Zeno make of riches, health, beauty, poverty, ill health and pain?

1.55

They are advantageous (health, riches, beauty) or disadvantageous (ill health, poverty, pain), but not good or evil.

40. Whose side does Cicero take, the Old Academy's or Zeno's?

1.55

The Academy's

41. What does Cicero assert the law should do?

1.58

Correct wickedness and promote goodness.

42. According to Cicero, what is the mother of all good things? 1.58 – Wisdom

43. According to Cicero, what is the best gift of the gods? 1.58 – Wisdom

44. What most difficult lesson does wisdom teach?

1.58

To know ourselves.

45. According to Cicero, what does the person who knows himself realize?

1.59

That he possesses something divine.

46. According to Cicero, to what does the person who knows himself compare his inner nature?

1.59

To a kind of holy image placed within a temple.

47. Why is the man who knows himself happy?

1.59

Because he realizes he has the makings of a good man.

48. According to Cicero, what does the mind do on perceiving the virtues?

1.60

It ceases to serve the body; expunges pleasure; leaves behind the fear of pain and death; enters loving fellowship with its own kind; and worships the gods; sharpens moral judgment.

49. According to Cicero, of what place is a man who knows himself a citizen?

1.61

Of the whole world as if it were a single city.

50. What does rhetoric allow the man who knows himself to do?

1.62

He can rule nations, reinforce laws, castigate the wicked, protect the good, praise eminent men, instruct in security and prestige, inspire honorable actions, restrain citizens from disgrace, console the afflicted, recount the deeds and counsels of brave and wise men, and recount the infamy of the wicked.

51. According to Cicero, what is the parent of those powers?

1.62

Wisdom

THE
LAWS
Book 2

LESSON XIV: The Laws, Book 2.1-22

TEACHING NOTES

Homework Questions: 3, 4, 5, 6, 7, 8, 9, 10, 12, 14, 15, 20, 21, 22, 27, 28, 30, 31

Quiz Questions: 3, 4, 6, 14, 15, 21

Discussion Focus Questions: 2

SYNOPSIS

Book 2.1-22 Cicero's Religious Law Code

1-7 Double citizenship

8-14 Natural law and civil law

14-18 Introduction to the law

19-22 Cicero's ideal law code: religious laws
    19 Which gods should be worshiped
    19-20 Ritual calendar
    20-21 Priesthoods
    21-22 Religious prohibitions
    22 Obligations to the deceased and funerary regulations

I. THOUGHT QUESTIONS:

1. What is wrong with Cicero's argument that reason and natural law account for the actions of Tarquin and Horatius? What would it need to make it work?

2. Cicero asserts that some rules laid down by societies are just, and therefore true laws, and some are unjust, and therefore undeserving of the name of law, but he does not address how a person should act who does not live in his utopia of perfectly just civil law. Let us assume that some of our laws are just and some unjust. Should citizens obey unjust laws? Come up with three reasons and one scenario to support each side of this question.

II. COMPREHENSION QUESTIONS:

1. According to Cicero, what two sorts of citizenships can a person have?

   2.5

   Local and legal

2. According to Cicero, which kind of citizenship should have "first place in our affections"?

   2.5

   The state (legal citizenship). We should be willing to die for it, should devote ourselves

   to it heart and soul, and dedicate and consecrate all that is ours on its altar.

3. According to Cicero, on what must laws be founded? _____ 2.8 – Reason

4. According to Cicero, from where does law *not* come?

   2.8

   Not from the intelligence of human beings, or from resolutions passed by communities.

5. According to Cicero, from where does law come?

   2.8

   It is an eternal force which rules the world by the wisdom of its commands and prohibitions.

6. According to Cicero, what is the original and final law?

   2.8

   The intelligence of God, who ordains or forbids everything by reason.

7. According to Cicero, what does civil law have the power to do?

   2.9

   Encourage people to right actions and deter them from wrongdoing.

8. According to Cicero, where does civil law originate?

   2.9-2.10

   It is coeval with that god who watches over and rules heaven and earth.

9. How does Cicero explain the good actions of Horatius and the bad actions of Tarquin, which were outside civil law?

   2.10

   Reason exists outside of law. Reason is derived from the nature of the universe and

   impels people to right actions and restrains them from wrong.

10. According to Cicero, why is civil law called law?

    2.11

    Because of popular approval rather than actual fact.

11. According to Cicero, to what ends were civil laws devised?

2.11

To ensure the safety of citizens, the security of states, and the peaceful, happy life of human beings.

12. According to Cicero, what should not be called laws?

2.11

Harmful and unjust rules

13. According to Cicero, why is law a good thing?

2.12

The lack of law prevents a state from being called a state.

Note: *As stated, this is a bizarrely fallacious argument. It could stand with support, but Cicero gives it none.*

14. According to Cicero, what should be the measure of whether a law is just or unjust?

2.13 – Nature

15. How did Plato believe laws should be accepted?

2.14

By consent rather than threats of violence.

16. According to Cicero, why should citizens take note of the pious and the impious?

2.15-2.16

Minds imbued with these facts will surely not deviate from true and wholesome ideas.

17. According to Cicero, who should not be counted as human?

2.16

Anyone who does not give thanks for the procession of the stars, day and night, the succession of the seasons, and the fruits of the earth.

18. According to Cicero, why does it have to be admitted that universal nature possesses intelligence?

2.16

Everything with intelligence is superior to everything that lacks it, and nothing is superior to universal nature.

Note: *This is a fallacious syllogism. See Explanatory Notes on terminology in the text.*

19. How does the reader know that Cicero considers wealth impure?

2.19

He asserts that to be pure and holy, wealth must be set aside.

20. According to Cicero, what gods should be worshiped?

2.19 – Whether public or private, only the gods handed down by the forefathers and those officially recognized should be worshiped.

Note: This leaves no room whatsoever for religions (like ours) that expect any sort of proselytizing or conversion, as they necessarily require the abandonment of the forefathers' religions in favor of the new creed. You could use this to make a shallow argument for those whose forefathers were Christian, but it leaves no room for new conversions, for the initial conversion of the forefathers, or even for Protestantism, so I would steer students away from applying this to Christianity. As an interesting parallel, Ghandi also felt that an individual should not depart from the religion in which he was raised, no matter what it might be, but strive to be faithful to the religion of his fathers.

21. According to Cicero's laws, what should be worshiped in addition to the gods?

2.19

Men who have become gods and the qualities that allow men to become gods.

22. According to Cicero's laws, how can humans ascend to heaven?

2.19 – through good sense, moral excellence, devotion, and good faith.

Note: There were established temples to these virtues in Rome. Of course, there was also the temple to Libertas that Clodius Pulcher had established on the site of Cicero's house after he'd torn it down and had Cicero exiled, but, being a little bitter about this (deservedly), Cicero does not include Libertas on this list.

23. Describe the holidays as they are laid out in Cicero's laws.

2.19-2.20

There are no lawsuits; they are celebrated with the whole household, including slaves; priests offer sacrifices in public according to fixed rites on fixed days. The priests should arrange the schedule and type of offerings.

24. Describe the three priesthoods set out in Cicero's laws.

2.20-2.21

One kind presides over rites and ceremonies; one kind interprets prophecies; one kind divines the future through signs and omens (augurs).

25. According to Cicero's laws, what should happen to a person who fails to heed the advice of an augur?

2.21 – He should be killed.

Note: Cicero was an augur.

26. According to Cicero's laws, what should Etruscan soothsayers do?

2.21

Interpret portents, make sacrifices in expiation, and make atonement in response to lightning flashes.

27. According to Cicero's laws, what is the only nocturnal sacrifice allowed by women?

2.21 – The one at the Bona Dea festival

> Note: *No men were in attendance at the Bona Dea festival (except that one time with Clodius Pulcher, oops), so this is consistent with his later justification of this law as protecting women's reputations.*

28. According to Cicero, what is the only legal mystery?

2.21

The mysteries of Ceres*

29. Describe public entertainments according to Cicero's laws.

2.22

Music in honor of the gods is required when there are no chariot races and athletic competitions.

30. List the religious laws Cicero sets out which carry a punishment of death.

2.21-2.22 – disobeying augurs, stealing sacred objects or objects from sacred places, divine perjury, incest.

> Note: *Incest here may refer to the violation of chastity vows by the vestal virgins. See Explanatory Notes in text.*

31. For what non-Roman gods do Cicero's laws make provision?

2.21-2.22 – Bona Dea, Ceres, Cybele (Idaean Mother)

> Note: *Despite the bizarre and unsettling nature of the worship of Cybele, it was sanctioned by the senate during the Punic Wars because it was imported in response to a prophecy, and they decreed thanks to Cybele after the destruction of Carthage.*

32. According to Cicero's laws, who should be considered gods?

2.22

Dead good men

***Note:** Cicero includes the mysteries of Ceres because they were widespread, socially accepted, and, perhaps most importantly, he was an initiate of them. Other mysteries popular at the time included mysteries of Isis, Dionysus, Cybele, and Mithras (only practiced by men), all of which were significantly more controversial and counter-cultural than those of Ceres. Although substantially different in some important respects, early Christianity in Rome was practiced in a similar manner to the existing mystery religions of the time. In Rome, mystery religions were generally relatively secret, required some sort of initiation such as baptism, tended to be centered around rituals, and often implied a personal relationship with a deity. They were also foreign, hence Cicero's distrust. Early Christianity would have been forbidden under this law (not that it was legal anyway). Beyond the inherent fun of a secret, their popularity can be partially attested to the personal nature of these religions. They stand in contrast to the state-centered nature of public Roman religion, as well as the private family religion, in which the state or the family is the focus, and the individual has little beyond obligation. They provided to the individual a sense of purpose, worth, and hope of union with a god beyond death, regardless of social standing, and so they were particularly popular with women and the plebs. Cicero's system, and really all his philosophy, hinges on the strict preservation of the proper hierarchy (with himself near the top, of course) of slaves, women, freedmen, plebs, equites, patricians, statesmen, consuls, ancestors, and gods. There is no room in this for any individuality; your worth is determined by your obedience to the system. Hence, it is no wonder that Cicero so distrusted the mystery cults. Bear in mind also that as a member of the Skeptic school, he condemns much of religion as superstition except what supports the state and the institutions necessary for its integrity (e.g., the family). Most Skeptics went considerably further. Remember that Socrates was executed for corrupting the youth by causing them to doubt the gods.*

LESSON XV: The Laws, Book 2.23-69

TEACHING NOTES

Homework Questions: 1, 2, 3, 6, 9, 11, 13, 14, 15, 16, 17, 19, 25, 26, 27, 28

Quiz Questions: 4, 11, 13, 17, 26

Discussion Focus Questions: 1

SYNOPSIS

Book 2.23-69 Commentary on Cicero's Religious Law Code

23-68 Commentary on Cicero's ideal religious laws

    23-24 Introduction

    24-28 Worship

    29 Ritual calendar

    29-34 Priesthoods

    35-45 Religious prohibitions

    45-68 Obligations to the deceased and funerary regulations

69 Conclusion

I. THOUGHT QUESTIONS:

1. Cicero claims that a state is held together by the people's need for the advice and authority of the aristocracy. However, American society has no strict or legally instituted social classes. As a result, we have no need to rely on the advice of aristocrats, nor do we have aristocrats on whom to rely. And yet (in defiance of Cicero's assertion) our state holds together. What do you think holds the United States together? What do you think should hold it together?

2. Do you think binding factors are unique to each nation or society, or are they universal?

II. COMPREHENSION QUESTIONS:

1. What sort of laws does Cicero add to existing Roman law?

   2.23

   Only those which are traditional.

2. How does Cicero define "purity"?

   2.24

   Purity is of both the body (which is easily washed) and the heart (whose impurities are not washed away and do not fade with time).

   Note: *Obviously a pre-Christian view with no grace whatsoever.*

3. According to Cicero, why should adopting a spirit of holiness require setting aside wealth?

   2.25

   Extravagance is not pleasing to God because it prevents the poor from worshiping him.

4. What is Cicero's objection to foreign gods and new gods?

   2.25-2.26 – They cause confusion because the rites are unfamiliar. **Note:** *I seriously doubt this was his real reason. As a strong conservative with a broad nostalgic streak, Cicero was deeply uncomfortable with everything both foreign and new, possibly because it had the potential to upset the traditional hierarchy on which he hung his utopian state. However, he is too pious a man to say that other gods are not as real or as powerful or as important as the gods of Rome, or that they would be problematic in themselves, so he avoids the issue by claiming that he is merely avoiding confusion for the priesthood.*

5. Why does Cicero believe there should be shrines in cities and groves in the countryside?

   2.26

   So that the people living in the same places as the gods would be more pure in heart.

6. Why does Cicero believe that one should only practice religion that is handed down?

   2.27

   He believes that the further back one goes in time, the nearer one gets to the gods.

7. Which traditional aspects of Roman religion does Cicero reject?

   2.28

   Those which recognize things he believes should be rejected, specifically fever and evil fortune.

   Note: *Regarding this practice, these were probably less honored than warded off through religious bribery.*

8. According to Cicero, what two functions should the vestal virgins serve?

   2.29

   They should maintain the fire and act as examples of chastity for other women.

9. According to Cicero, what holds the state together?

2.30 – The people's continual need of the advice and authority of the aristocracy.

> Note: *This is not in any way an accurate portrayal of the patron-client system or other interactions between Roman social classes. The patron-client system was an exchange for mutual benefit. In casting the plebs as perpetual children, Cicero portrays them as dependent on the aristocracy rather than acknowledging the complex interdependence of real relationships between the classes in republican Rome.*

10. According to Cicero, why is the power of the augurs the most prestigious in the state?

2.31

Because it includes political authority; they can dismiss assemblies, cancel decision, ask consuls to resign, and annul laws.

11. Why does Cicero, a Skeptic and follower of Plato, believe in divination?

2.32-2.33

1 - Logic: The gods are real; they rule the world; they have the power to give signs; they care for mankind.

2 - He claims history bears out the predictions of past augurs.

12. Why does Cicero think the skill of augury vanished?

2.33

As a result of age and neglect.

13. According to Cicero, what should be the most important factors in all aspects of a war?

2.34

Justice and good faith

14. Why does Cicero approve of the Eleusinian mysteries?

2.36

He himself was an initiate; he believes they made men civilized; they taught ways to live happily and die well.

15. Why does Cicero prohibit nocturnal sacrifices by women?

2.36-2.37 – The bad reputation that they have from plays; the affair with Clodius Pulcher at the Bona Dea festival; women's reputations would be preserved.

> Note: *It is particularly interesting that he would rather condemn women's sacrifices than condemn the (apparent) sacrilege of playwrights. He gives much credence to crass jokes, and very little to women's self-control.*

16. Why does Cicero believe there should be music and singing at public games?

2.38

Music influences people by manipulating the emotions.

17. What does Cicero find disturbing about the contemporary music of his day?

2.39

People swaying and nodding their heads in time with the music.

18. What traditions does Cicero claim are the best?

2.40

The oldest and (ergo) nearest to God.

19. Why does Cicero forbid religions from soliciting or collecting money?

2.40

Such practices fill men's minds with superstitions and empty their pockets.

20. How does Cicero claim he saved his country?

2.42

By preventing a statue of Minerva from being defiled.

21. According to Cicero, what is divine punishment?

2.44

In life, the disturbance of the mind through guilt

In death, such infamy that the living rejoice at their destruction

22. Why does Cicero believe fields ought not be consecrated?

2.45

According to Plato, the earth is already sacred. Cicero also believes that superstition will lead to a decline in agriculture.

23. What materials did Plato deem worthy and unworthy for an offering to a god?

2.45

Worthy: wood (of one piece), stone, textile (less than 1 month's labor and preferably white), pictures (no more than can be painted by one artist in one day), birds (most holy)

Unworthy: gold and silver (arouse envy), ivory (unclean because it comes from a carcass), bronze and iron (they are the paraphernalia of war)

Note: *Plato's ideal was grossly inconsistent with actual Greek religious practice. The main cult statues of Zeus at Olympia and Athena in the Parthenon were both of gold and ivory, bronze statues and votives were common, along with elaborate works of art. Soldiers, and particularly victorious generals, devoted weapons and armor to gods in thanksgiving. Also, some Greek gods were warlike. It would be bizarre to say that it is impious to dedicate bronze to Athena because it is used in war when she herself was a goddess of war. It is important to remember that Plato had strong (and important) opinions about many things, but he did not make the actual rules.*

24. Why did Cicero's laws specify that traditional rites should be continued in perpetuity?

2.47-2.48

So they should not be forgotten when a paterfamilias (father of a family) dies.

25. Why do those who inherit property bear the responsibility for rites in honor of the deceased?

2.48-2.49

The rites were expensive, so they should follow the material inheritance.

Note: *There was apparently a huge problem with the contemporary Roman system.*

26. Why does Cicero believe pontiffs should not be involved in or knowledgeable of civil law?

2.52-2.53

Because they can use it to circumvent religious authority and obligations (for example, the rites of the deceased).

27. What form of burial does Cicero believe to be the most ancient?

2.56 – inhumation Note: *While earlier inhumation was indicated by the Roman custom of cutting off the finger to be buried when a body was cremated, cremation is mentioned in both the Iliad and the Odyssey, our earliest Greek mentions of any kind of burial. Moreover, archaeological evidence from early cemeteries indicates that, much like in modern America, both were practiced concurrently, although one or the other seemed to usually be more common. It is very unclear which is earlier.*

28. According to Cicero, why did Sulla specify that his body be cremated?

2.56-2.57

So that his remains could not be scattered the way he scattered Marius's remains.

29. When was a grave considered sacred?

2.57

When earth had been placed over bone and a pig had been slaughtered.

30. Why did those buried near the altar of honor need to be dug up before it could be dedicated as a temple?

2.58

A public place could not be made subject to the obligations associated with private religion. (Tombs are focal points of private religion, and temples are public places.)

Note: *When Cicero talks of God, it is easy to forget that he is a pagan and means Jupiter. This part of The Laws is a good reminder of just how different Roman thinking and religion were from ours.*

31. What limitations did the Twelve Tables place on funeral expenses?

2.59-2.60

They were limited to three veils, a small purple tunic, and ten pipers. They could not hold two funerals, be anointed by slaves, have drinking bouts, conduct expensive sprinkling with wine, wear chaplets of flowers, burn incense or add gold (to the grave).

32. Why does Cicero approve of the limitations placed on funeral expenses by the Twelve Tables?

2.59

"It is entirely in keeping with nature that differences in fortune should be abolished in death."

33. Describe Greek law regarding tombs.

2.64-2.66

They are not to be destroyed, damaged, or knocked down. Outsiders are not to be buried in them. No one should build a tomb which it took ten men longer than three days to complete. Stucco and herms were forbidden. Funeral speeches were only allowed at public funerals by an official. Crowds were prohibited. Later, they had to be held before dawn, and graves could only be marked by a small pillar, a table, or a small bowl. In earlier times, grain was sown over the grave.

Note: *These laws are Athenian, not universal to the Greeks. Also, the sowing of grain is probably related to the Eleusinian mysteries of Demeter, which appear to have focused on the agricultural cycle as an explanation of death, possibly with a promise of rebirth. Because Athens was so close to Eleusis, a great many Athenians were initiates of those mysteries.*

34. Describe Plato's views on funerals.

2.67-2.68

Tombs cannot be on land that can be cultivated, but capable land should be filled to the maximum extent. He forbids tombs beyond what five men can build in five days. Any stone object larger than required for four lines of hexameter is prohibited. Funerals should cost between one and five minae.

THE
LAWS
Book 3

LESSON XVI: The Laws, Book 3.1-32

TEACHING NOTES

Homework Questions: 2, 4, 6, 14, 16, 17, 19, 20, 21, 22, 23, 27, 28, 30, 31, 33, 34

Quiz Questions: 16, 17, 19, 22, 23, 31, 33

Discussion Focus Questions: 3, 4

SYNOPSIS

Book 3.1-32 Cicero's Ideal Laws: Magistrates

    1-5 Introduction and current laws concerning magistrates

    6-11 Cicero's law code: magistrates

    12-32 Commentary on Cicero's law code concerning magistrates

        12-17 Variations from Greece and Rome

        17-19 Ambassadors and embassies

        19-26 The tribunate

        27-32 The senate

I. THOUGHT QUESTIONS:

1. What can you infer about meetings of the Senate in late Republican Rome based on sections 3.10-3.11?

2. What can you infer about meetings of the Assemblies in late Republican Rome based on sections 3.10-3.11?

3. Sections 3.28-3.30 indicate a great deal of corruption in the Senate. Cicero does not include any new measures to prevent corruption; rather, he asserts that the contemporary systems ought to work. Cicero overcomes Atticus's protests by saying that this system is ideal and not meant to take on the present. Unfortunately, corruption is not a political problem isolated to the Roman republic, but is an ailment common to many forms of government. How would you prevent and address the issue of corruption in the ruling bodies of a government?

4. Cicero seems to believe that men who have not been corrupt before entering office will not be corrupt in positions of power. Do you agree? Why or why not? How would you monitor officials to the benefit of the public?

II. COMPREHENSION QUESTIONS:

1. According to Cicero, what is a magistrate's function?

   3.2

   To take charge and to issue directives which are right, beneficial, and in accordance with the laws.

2. According to Cicero, "a magistrate is a _____ speaking law _____, and law a _____ silent magistrate   (3.2) _____."

3. What do the house, the state, the clan, the human race, nature, and the whole universe need to survive?

   3.3

   Authority

4. According to Cicero, how does one show his aptitude for wielding power?

   3.5

   By quietly executing the orders of others.

5. According to Cicero, what are the people's duties to the magistrate?

   3.5

   To obey them and carry out their instructions, and also to give them honor and esteem.

6. What did Plato think of citizens who oppose magistrates?

   3.5

   He thought they were descended from the Titans, who themselves opposed the gods.

7. According to Cicero, what should be the powers of magistrates at home?

   3.6

   They shall punish the guilty and unruly by fine, prison, or flogging; the accused have the right to appeal; the magistrate makes the decision of guilt and the people fix the penalty.

   They watch over public funds; they ensure the security of prisoners; they watch over public funds and mint coins; they judge cases and carry out whatever the Senate decides.

8. According to Cicero, what should be the powers of the magistrate in the field?

   3.6

   The orders of the commanding officer are final; there is no appeal; minor magistrates have authority in their own spheres; they command and function as tribunes for those under them.

9. Describe the office of aedile according to Cicero.

3.7

They look after matters in the city, including food supply and public entertainments.

10. Describe the office of censor according to Cicero.

3.7

They take the census, watch over temples, streets, and aqueducts, watch over the treasury and taxes, assign the citizens to tribes, divide the tribes into classes by wealth, age, and rank. They force men to marry and remove the disreputable from the Senate. There should be two censors in five-year terms.

11. Describe the office of praetor according to Cicero.

3.8

They should decide civil cases and guard civil law.

12. Describe the office of consul according to Cicero.

3.8

Leading, judging, consulting, supreme military powers, highest authority.

13. Describe the office of dictator according to Cicero.

3.9

Only during serious or civil war there should be a dictator for six months or less. The dictator's power is equal to two consuls; the dictator should be appointed by the Senate under favorable auspices. He shall have an officer to command the cavalry (with authority equal to that of a praetor).

14. What restrictions does Cicero place on all magistrates?

3.9

They should not hold the same office more than one time every ten years; they shall leave the city if the Senate or people command it; they shall conduct just wars in a just manner; treat allies with consideration; control themselves and their staff; increase glory of their country and return home with honor.

15. Describe the office of tribune according to Cicero.

3.9

There are ten tribunes appointed by the plebs to protect them from violence; they have the power of veto; what they enact through the plebs is binding; they are sacrosanct.

16. What powers does Cicero reserve for all magistrates?

3.10

The right to take auspices, conduct trials, and veto the decrees of lower magistrates.

17. According to Cicero, who should appoint the magistrates? 3.10 – The people

18. According to Cicero, which magistrates should have the right to preside over meetings of the people and the Senate?

3.10

Consuls, praetors, dictators, master of the cavalry, any official proposed by the Senate for conducting the election of consuls, tribunes.

19. According to Cicero, how should meetings of the Senate be conducted?

3.10-3.11

They should be conducted with decent restraint. Senators should be punished for unexcused absences. Senators must speak in turn and briefly. They should have a grasp of public affairs.

20. According to Cicero, how should meetings of the people be conducted?

3.11

They should be free from violence; a higher magistrate (than the one presiding over the meeting) can overrule their decrees; auspices should be read and heeded; bills should be kept on record; votes should be on one question at a time; the people should be informed about what they are voting on; no laws should be directed at individuals (privilegia).

21. What were the first two steps in the reduction of consular power?

3.16

The tribunes are not bound by consular authority.

The tribunes lend support to those who flout the consul's authority.

22. Why does Quintus call the birth of the tribunate "a great calamity"?

3.17

Because it took power from the aristocracy and empowered the people.

23. Why does Cicero disagree with Quintus?

3.17

Because unchecked consular power appears arrogant and oppressive.

24. What changes does Cicero include in his utopian laws that he unsuccessfully tried to make to the Roman constitution as consul?

3.18

He would like to abolish senatorial ambassadors. As it was, he was blocked by a tribune, but still managed to limit the term to one year.

25. Outline Quintus's objections to the tribunate.

3.19-3.22

It arose during a time of sedition; it is in opposition to the social hierarchy, causing turmoil and confusion; it limits the powers of the aristocracy. He gives examples of the Gracchi and from Cicero's issue with Curiatius and Clodius.
Tribunes have opposed Cicero in the past and he doesn't like them.

26. Why is Cicero willing to accept the "element of evil inherent in the office of tribune"?

3.23

Without that evil, we would not have the good which was the whole purpose of setting it up.

27. Outline Cicero's defense of the tribunate.

3.23-3.26

The power of the tribunes is less savage and violent than the power of the people.
It keeps the people from resenting the aristocracy by creating an illusion of equality.
It prevents future sedition.

28. On what two other parts of Cicero's law does the binding nature of senatorial decrees depend?

3.28

The Senate is made up of magistrates whom the people elect, leaving authority in the hands of the Senate and power in the hands of the people.

The Senate needs to behave well and set a good example.

29. How does Cicero propose to ensure the unblemished behavior of the Senate?

3.29

The censors shall monitor their behavior; those who are "blemished" shouldn't be elected; ... education and training (presumably for moral excellence).

30. "Just as the whole state is apt to be infected by _____the vicious desires of its leaders_____, so it is healed and set right by _____their restraint (3.30)_____."

31. What does Cicero assert is the primary problem with aristocratic corruption?

3.31

It leads to corruption in the other classes as well.

32. According to Cicero, why is it not possible to put a stop to the greed of the lower classes?

3.31

Those who ought to do so are guilty of the same greed.

33. To what does Plato attribute changes in the nature of the state?

3.32

Changes in the vocal style of its musicians.

34. To what does Cicero attribute changes in the nature of the state?

3.32

They mirror changes in the lives and lifestyle of the aristocracy.

35. According to Cicero, why are corrupt leaders a menace?

3.32

Because they corrupt others.

LESSON XVII: The Laws, Book 3.33-49

TEACHING NOTES

Homework Questions: All

Quiz Questions: 3, 4, 5, 9

Discussion Focus Questions: 4, 5, 6

SYNOPSIS

Book 3.33-49 Commentary on Cicero's Ideal Laws Concerning Magistrates

33-47 Commentary on Cicero's law code concerning magistrates

33-46 Laws concerning elections and ballots

46-47 Censorship

48-49 Conclusion

I. THOUGHT QUESTIONS:

1. List three major changes in the character and structure of the United States since the Revolutionary War. To what do you attribute each of these changes? Teacher Note: Some examples are listed below. These changes may seem easy to categorize as good or bad, but at the time were much more touchy and morally complex, akin to today's ongoing marriage or abortion debates. Ex. Writing the Constitution, women's suffrage, prohibition, abolition, civil rights, women working, etc.

2. To what do you generally attribute changes in the nature and character of states? Do good and bad changes have the same sources?

3. Is it better for votes to be open or secret? Come up with three reasons why and why not for both public elections and senatorial elections.

4. For Cicero, the modern phenomenon of issue-based elections was not even a consideration. He instead assumes that elections are based on popularity and moral character. Come up with 2-3 reasons why voting decisions should be based on issues, and 2-3 reasons why they should be based on character.

5. According to Cicero, it is better to obstruct a good proposal than to acquiesce in a bad one. What do you think? Should this rule of thumb (whichever way you decide it should go) apply equally to all proposals?

6. Cicero's laws require magistrates leaving office to make a report and account for their actions in office. Why would this be a good practice? Why would this be a harmful practice?

II. COMPREHENSION QUESTIONS:

1. Summarize Quintus's opinions on secret voting.

   3.34-3.37

2. Summarize Cicero's opinions on secret voting.

   3.38

   Note: *Give background information here on violence and gangs in Rome used for electoral intimidation. Be sure to mention Marian Law and Clodius Pulcher.*

3. According to Cicero, what three things should be required of senators?

   3.40

   That they be present at meetings of the Senate; that they speak in turn; that they be brief.

4. Under what circumstances does Cicero approve of long speeches?

   3.40

   When the Senate is going wrong and no one is attempting to save the situation; when an issue is exceptionally important.

5. According to Cicero, with what knowledge does a senator need to be equipped for his job?

   3.41

   Know the state of the country regarding troops, finances, allies, tributaries, laws, conditions, treaties; understand legislative procedure; be aware of the traditional precedent.

6. According to Cicero, what is the most important rule of the people's assemblies?

3.42

There must be no violence.

7. How does a magistrate lose his *sacrosanctitas*?

3.42

By not closing a meeting when violence occurs.

8. What is *privilegium*?

3.44

A law passed against or for an individual.

9. Why does Cicero claim *privilegia* are unjust?

3.44

By definition, a law is something that applies to everyone.

10. According to Cicero, why should the Assembly of Centuries be allowed to pass *privilegia*?

3.44

He claims people think more carefully about their votes when they are split according to wealth, rank, and age (Also, the privilegium recalling Cicero from exile was passed by the Assembly of Centuries).

QUIZZES, EXAMS, & KEY

THE REPUBLIC: Lesson I Quiz

Name:_____ Date: _____ Score: _____

1. Why is law superior to philosophy? (2 pts.)

    _____

    _____

    _____

2. List the arguments made against taking part in public life, and Cicero's refutation of each (Questions 7 and 10 from the study guide). (10 pts.)

    Argument:

    _____

    _____

    Refutation:

    _____

    _____

    Argument:

    _____

    _____

    _____

    Refutation:

    _____

    _____

    _____

    Argument:

    _____

    _____

    Refutation:

    _____

    _____

    Argument:

    _____

    _____

    _____

Refutation:

_____

_____

_____

Argument:

_____

_____

Refutation:

_____

_____

_____

3. What claim does Cicero assert a country makes on its citizens? (4 pts.)

_____

_____

_____

_____

4. Why does Cicero believe that classical philosophers who did not hold office perform an important public function? (2 pts.)

_____

_____

5. What human virtue does Cicero believe most closely approaches the divine? (2 pts.)

_____

_____

_____

THE REPUBLIC: Lesson I Quiz – KEY

Name:_____ Date: _____ Score: _____

20 pts.

1. Why is law superior to philosophy? (2 pts.)

   1.3
   _____

   The law compels everyone to do what philosophy can persuade only a few people to do.
   _____

2. List the arguments made against taking part in public life and Cicero's refutation of each (Questions 7 and 10 from the study guide). (10 pts.)

   Argument:

   The labor it takes to defend the commonwealth.
   _____

   Refutation:

   It is a minor burden for an alert and vigorous man.
   _____

   Argument:

   The danger to one's life (supported by examples of political/military disasters such as
   Miltiades or Themistocles).
   _____

   Refutation:

   To fear death is disgraceful. Death is inevitable, and it is far more miserable to be worn
   away by nature and old age than to lay down one's life for one's country.
   _____

   Argument:

   The danger of exile, including Cicero's exile as an example.
   _____

   Refutation:

   Those who make these arguments also went overseas during the civil wars.
   _____

   Argument:

   Those who take part in public life are worthless men; to be paired with them is low, and
   to fight against them is dangerous.
   _____

Refutation:

   Good and brave men should not allow themselves to be subject to wicked men or
   allow wicked men to ravage the commonwealth while they are capable of helping it.

Argument:

   A wise man will take no part in public affairs unless a crisis compels him.

Refutation:

   It is impossible to bring aid to the state in a crisis if you are not already in a position to
   do so.

3. What claim does Cicero assert a country makes on its citizens? (4 pts.)

   1.8

   She has a claim on the largest and best part of our minds, talents, loyalty, and
   judgment for her own use, and leaves us for our private use only so much as is
   beyond her requirements.

4. Why does Cicero believe that classical philosophers who did not hold office perform an important
   public function? (2 pts.)

   1.12

   They did much research and writing about government.

5. What human virtue does Cicero believe most closely approaches the divine? (2 pts.)

   1.12

   Founding new states or preserving existing ones.

THE REPUBLIC: Participants in the Dialogue Quiz

Name:_____ Date: _____ Score: _____

9 pts.

1. _____ a legal expert

2. _____ Scipio's nephew and an eager student of philosophy

3. _____ a man of great personal rectitude who nevertheless takes on the defense
of injustice for the sake of argument

4. _____ The destroyer of Carthage; an extraordinary general who did not threaten
the state as the great generals of Cicero's time did. He was known to patronize writers. In the dialogue,
he appears as an idealist and theoretician, much like Cicero himself.

5. _____ conservative, anti-democracy

6. _____ a friend of Scipio's: politically cautious, practical, and down-to-earth

7. _____ a young participant in the dialogue

8. _____ a young participant in the dialogue

9. _____ a young participant in the dialogue

THE REPUBLIC: Participants in the Dialogue Quiz – KEY

Name:_____ Date: _____ Score: _____

9 pts.

1. ___Manilius_____ a legal expert

2. ___Tubero_____ Scipio's nephew and an eager student of philosophy

3. ___Philus_____ a man of great personal rectitude who nevertheless takes on the defense of injustice for the sake of argument

4. ___Scipio_____ The destroyer of Carthage; an extraordinary general who did not threaten the state as the great generals of Cicero's time did. He was known to patronize writers. In the dialogue, he appears as an idealist and theoretician, much like Cicero himself.

5. ___Mummius_____ conservative, anti-democracy

6. ___Laelius_____ a friend of Scipio's: politically cautious, practical, and down-to-earth

7. ___Rutilius_____ a young participant in the dialogue

8. ___Fannius_____ a young participant in the dialogue

9. ___Scaevola_____ a young participant in the dialogue

THE REPUBLIC: Lesson 2 Quiz

Name:_____ Date: _____ Score: _____

10 pts.

1. Why was Scipio impressed by Galus? (2 pts.)

_____

_____

_____

_____

_____

2. Who does Scipio say was the first to recognize eclipses? (1 pt.)

_____

_____

_____

3. Who does Scipio believe is the worst kind of person? (1 pt.)

_____

_____

_____

4. How does Scipio define the common law of nature regarding possession? (1 pt.)

_____

_____

_____

_____

5. Who does Scipio say is the wealthiest man? (1 pt.)

_____

_____

_____

6. Who does Scipio say is the most powerful man? (1 pt.)

_____

_____

_____

7. Who does Scipio say is the most blessed man? (1 pt.)

_____

_____

_____

8. Who does Scipio say is the man of the most secure good fortune? (1 pt.)

_____

_____

_____

9. What does Laelius say Scipio believed to be the best condition of the state? (1 pt.)

_____

_____

_____

THE REPUBLIC: Lesson 2 Quiz – KEY

Name:_____ Date: _____ Score: _____

10 pts.

1. Why was Scipio impressed by Galus? (2 pts.)

   1.23

   Galus had been able to convince the troops to set aside their fear at an eclipse by
   explaining it as a natural and scientific phenomenon rather than a portent of ill luck
   from the gods.

2. Who does Scipio say was the first to recognize eclipses? (1 pt.)

   1.25

   Thales of Miletus

3. Who does Scipio believe is the worst kind of person? (1 pt.)

   1.27

   Often the worst kind of person has possessions and power in limitless quantities.

4. How does Scipio define the common law of nature regarding possession? (1 pt.)

   1.27

   It forbids anything to belong to anyone except someone who knows how to employ
   and use it.

5. Who does Scipio say is the wealthiest man? (1 pt.)

   1.28

   The man who lacks nothing of what nature requires.

6. Who does Scipio say is the most powerful man? (1 pt.)

   1.28

   The man who achieves all that he seeks.

7. Who does Scipio say is the most blessed man? (1 pt.)

   1.28

   The man who is freed from emotional disturbance.

8. Who does Scipio say is the man of the most secure good fortune? (1 pt.)

1.28

The man who possesses only what he can carry with him out of a shipwreck.

9. What does Laelius say Scipio believed to be the best condition of the state? (1 pt.)

1.34

The one handed down by the ancestors.

THE REPUBLIC: Lesson 3 Quiz

Name:_____ Date: _____ Score: _____

13 pts.

1. Describe an early town and an early city in Scipio's model. (4 pts.)

   _____

   _____

   _____

2. Which form of government does Scipio say is least desirable? (1 pt.)

   _____

   _____

3. What kind of government does Scipio say is most to be desired? (1 pt.)

   _____

   _____

4. What would the citizens whom Scipio calls free in name only need to be free, and why are they not? (4 pts.)

   _____

   _____

   _____

   _____

5. How does discord arise in a state? (2 pts.)

   _____

   _____

6. What holds a community of citizens together? (1 pts.)

   _____

   _____

   _____

THE REPUBLIC: Lesson 3 Quiz – KEY

Name:_____ Date: _____ Score: _____

13 pts.

1. Describe an early town and an early city in Scipio's model. (4 pts.)

   1.41
   _____
   town: consists of homes protected by fortifications
   _____
   city: a town which includes shrines and common spaces
   _____

2. Which form of government does Scipio say is least desirable? (1 pt.)

   1.42
   _____
   Rule by the people
   _____

3. What kind of government does Scipio say is most to be desired? (1 pt.)

   1.45
   _____
   One that is blended from the three basic types (monarchy, oligarchy, democracy).
   _____

4. What would the citizens whom Scipio calls free in name only need to be free, and why are they not? (4 pts.)

   1.47
   _____
   They would need political power, political voice, and judiciary power, but these things
   _____
   are apportioned on the basis of birth or wealth.
   _____

5. How does discord arise in a state? (2 pts.)

   1.49
   _____
   It arises from incompatible interests, when different policies suit different people.
   _____

6. What holds a community of citizens together? (1 pts.)

   1.49
   _____
   Equality under the law
   _____

THE REPUBLIC: Lesson 4 Quiz

Name:_____ Date: _____ Score: _____

14 pts.

1. What does Scipio say is always a risk? (2 pts.)

_____

_____

_____

2. Why does Scipio say it is hard to choose which system of government is best? (6 pts.)

_____

_____

_____

_____

_____

3. Why does Scipio assert that religion support monarchy? (2 pts.)

_____

_____

_____

_____

4. Who do the Greeks say are barbarians? (1 pt.)

_____

_____

_____

5. According to Scipio, what does monarchy turn into, and why? (2 pts.)

_____

_____

_____

6. What does Scipio say turns any rule into its opposite? (1 pt.)

_____

_____

_____

THE REPUBLIC: Lesson 4 Quiz – KEY

Name:_____ Date:_____ Score:_____

14 pts.

1. What does Scipio say is always a risk? (2 pts.)

   1.53

   That equality before the law cannot be maintained indefinitely.

   _____

2. Why does Scipio say it is hard to choose which system of government is best? (6 pts.)

   1.55

   - Kings attract us by affection.
   - Aristocracies attract us by good sense.
   - Democracies attract us by freedom.

   _____

3. Why does Scipio assert that religion support monarchy? (2 pts.)

   1.56

   He says there is one king in heaven who is regarded as the king and father of all, and
   all gods are ruled by one divine power.

   _____

4. Who do the Greeks say are barbarians? (1 pt.)

   1.58

   All people other than Greeks.

   _____

5. According to Scipio, what does monarchy turn into, and why? (2 pts.)

   1.65

   It turns into tyranny because of injustice.

   _____

6. What does Scipio say turns any rule into its opposite? (1 pt.)

   1.68

   Excess

   _____

THE REPUBLIC: Lesson 5 Quiz

Name: _____ Date: _____ Score: _____

11 pts.

1. How is Cicero (through Scipio) breaking from the tradition of Socrates and Plato? (2 pts.)

   _____

   _____

   _____

2. What are the Fathers? (1 pt.)

   _____

   _____

   _____

3. What political institutions did Romulus and Tatius establish? (2 pts.)

   _____

   _____

   _____

4. Who received the plunder from Romulus's wars? (2 pts.)

   _____

   _____

   _____

5. What act marked the beginning of the Roman state? (1 pt.)

   _____

   _____

   _____

6. What form did early Roman wealth take? (2 pts.)

   _____

   _____

   _____

7. Who is Quirinus? (1 pt.)

   _____

   _____

   _____

THE REPUBLIC: Lesson 5 Quiz – KEY

Name:_____ Date: _____ Score: _____

11 pts.

1. How is Cicero (through Scipio) breaking from the tradition of Socrates and Plato? (2 pts.)

   2.3

   By describing the development of a real state rather than an imaginary community.

2. What are the Fathers? (1 pt.)

   2.14

   A royal council made up of leading citizens.

3. What political institutions did Romulus and Tatius establish? (2 pts.)

   2.14

   They established the Fathers, and they divided the populus into three tribes and into thirty voting districts.

4. Who received the plunder from Romulus's wars? (2 pts.)

   2.15

   Only the citizens, not Romulus himself.

5. What act marked the beginning of the Roman state? (1 pt.)

   2.16

   Romulus taking auspices before founding the city.

6. What form did early Roman wealth take? (2 pts.)

   2.16

   Livestock and land

7. Who is Quirinus? (1 pt.)

   2.20

   The deified Romulus

THE REPUBLIC: Lesson 6 Quiz

Name:_____ Date: _____ Score: _____

13 pts.

1. What are Patricians? (1 pt.)

_____

_____

_____

2. What did the early Romans look for in a king? (3 pts.)

_____

_____

_____

3. What things provide the most favorable conditions for the growth of justice and good faith? (2 pts.)

_____

_____

_____

4. How did Numa win the fierce and brutal Romans over to civilized behavior? (3 pts.)

_____

_____

_____

5. According to Scipio, what two factors ensure that states will last? (2 pts.)

_____

_____

_____

6. What important point did the early kings of Rome grasp? (2 pts.)

_____

_____

_____

THE REPUBLIC: Lesson 6 Quiz – KEY

Name:_____ Date: _____ Score: _____

13 pts.

1. What are Patricians? (1 pt.)

   2.23
   _____

   The children of the Fathers
   _____

   _____

2. What did the early Romans look for in a king? (3 pts.)

   2.23
   _____

   Valor and good sense rather than noble lineage.
   _____

   _____

3. What things provide the most favorable conditions for the growth of justice and good faith? (2 pts.)

   2.26
   _____

   Peace and relaxation
   _____

   _____

4. How did Numa win the fierce and brutal Romans over to civilized behavior? (3 pts.)

   2.27
   _____

   He instituted fairs, games, and other public gatherings.
   _____

   _____

5. According to Scipio, what two factors ensure that states will last? (2 pts.)

   2.27
   _____

   Religion and humane behavior
   _____

   _____

6. What important point did the early kings of Rome grasp? (2 pts.)

   2.31
   _____

   Certain rights should be granted to the people.
   _____

   _____

THE REPUBLIC: Lesson 7 Quiz

Name:_____ Date: _____ Score: _____

15 pts.

1. How did Servius Tullius rearrange the Assemblies to take power away from the people? (2 pts.)

_____

_____

_____

_____

2. Who are the assidui? (1 pt.)

_____

_____

_____

3. Who are the proletarii? (1 pt.)

_____

_____

_____

4. How does Scipio define freedom? (2 pts.)

_____

_____

_____

5. Why did the people initially put up with Tarquinius Superbus even though he was harsh and unjust? (2 pts.)

_____

_____

_____

6. To preserve a government from change, the magistrates must have _____,

the aristocratic council _____, and the people _____. (3 pts.)

7. How did the people originally get tribunes elected? (2 pts.)

_____

_____

_____

8. To what does Scipio compare reason? (2 pts.)

_____

_____

_____

THE REPUBLIC: Lesson 7 Quiz – KEY

Name:_____ Date: _____ Score: _____

15 pts.

1. How did Servius Tullius rearrange the Assemblies to take power away from the people? (2 pts.)

   2.39

   He organized them into five classes, and distributed them in such a way that most

   votes were in the hands of the wealthy.

2. Who are the assidui? (1 pt.)

   2.40

   The rich

3. Who are the proletarii? (1 pt.)

   2.40

   The poor

4. How does Scipio define freedom? (2 pts.)

   2.43

   Having no master at all, even a just one.

5. Why did the people initially put up with Tarquinius Superbus even though he was harsh and unjust? (2 pts.)

   2.44

   His military success brought wealth into Rome.

6. To preserve a government from change, the magistrates must have _____adequate power (2.57)__,

   the aristocratic council ____adequate influence____, and the people __adequate freedom__. (3 pts.)

7. How did the people originally get tribunes elected? (2 pts.)

   2.58-2.59

   Through seditious (rebellious) action.

8. To what does Scipio compare reason? (2 pts.)

   2.67

   A man who controls an elephant while riding it.

THE REPUBLIC: Lesson 8 Quiz

Name:_____ Date: _____ Score: _____

9 pts.

1. If forced to choose between scholarship and statecraft, which course does Cicero recommend? (1 pt.)

   _____

   _____

2. According to Philus, what is the simplest way of getting at the truth? (1 pt.)

   _____

   _____

   _____

3. What does Philus contend is the weakness of Plato and Aristotle in advocating justice? (2 pts.)

   _____

   _____

   _____

4. If justice were part of nature, it would be _____ for _____. (1 pt.)

5. According the Philus, how would things be different if justice were a function of nature? (2 pts.)

   _____

   _____

   _____

   _____

6. According to Philus, what causes the compromise of mixed government? (2 pts.)

   _____

   _____

   _____

THE REPUBLIC: Lesson 8 Quiz – KEY

Name:_____ Date: _____ Score: _____

9 pts.

1. If forced to choose between scholarship and statecraft, which course does Cicero recommend? (1 pt.)

   3.6

   Statecraft

2. According to Philus, what is the simplest way of getting at the truth? (1 pt.)

   3.8

   Arguing both sides of a case.

3. What does Philus contend is the weakness of Plato and Aristotle in advocating justice? (2 pts.)

   3.13

   Justice is a political phenomenon, not an element in nature.

4. If justice were part of nature, it would be ____the same____ for ____everyone (3.13)____. (1 pt.)

5. According the Philus, how would things be different if justice were a function of nature? (2 pts.)

   3.18

   Every country would have the same laws, and one country would not have different laws at different times.

6. According to Philus, what causes the compromise of mixed government? (2 pts.)

   3.23

   Mutual fear between classes and individuals.

THE REPUBLIC: Lesson 9 Quiz

Name:_____ Date: _____ Score: _____

11 pts.

1. What makes a war just or unjust? (4 pts.)

    _____

    _____

    _____

    _____

    _____

2. According to Laelius, over what does the mind rule like a king over subjects? (1 pt.)

    _____

    _____

    _____

3. According to Laelius, over what does the mind rule like a master crushing the spirits of his slaves? (2 pts.)

    _____

    _____

    _____

4. Why does a good man not seek incentives such as power and kingdoms? (2 pts.)

    _____

    _____

    _____

5. Why does Scipio refuse to call Syracuse a republic? (2 pts.)

    _____

    _____

    _____

THE REPUBLIC: Lesson 9 Quiz – KEY

Name:_____ Date: _____ Score: _____

11 pts.

1. What makes a war just or unjust? (4 pts.)

   3.35

   A war is just if it is undertaken without proper cause; for any reason other than

   repelling an enemy or for punishing an enemy; it must be declared and proclaimed;

   redress (presumably non-violent) must have been previously sought.

2. According to Laelius, over what does the mind rule like a king over subjects? (1 pt.)

   3.37

   The body

3. According to Laelius, over what does the mind rule like a master crushing the spirits of his slaves? (2 pts.)

   3.37

   Desire and anger

4. Why does a good man not seek incentives such as power and kingdoms? (2 pts.)

   3.40

   Because they are human possessions and he regards his own goods as divine.

5. Why does Scipio refuse to call Syracuse a republic? (2 pts.)

   3.43

   It is ruled by one man, and a republic is the property of the public.

THE REPUBLIC: Lesson 10 Quiz

Name:_____ Date: _____ Score: _____

10 pts.

1. According to Cicero, what two things are necessary for founding and maintaining a great empire? (2 pts.)

   _____

   _____

   _____

2. According to Cicero, how did his generation treat the mos maiorum? (3 pts.)

   _____

   _____

   _____

   _____

3. According to Cicero, why had Rome lost the name and substance of Republic? (1 pt.)

   _____

   _____

   _____

4. According to Scipio, in what two aspects of law does a statesman need to be versed? (2 pts.)

   _____

   _____

   _____

5. "No honest man can be corrupted by_____, but he *can* be corrupted by

   _____." (2 pts.)

THE REPUBLIC: Lesson 10 Quiz – KEY

Name:_____ Date: _____ Score: _____

10 pts.

1. According to Cicero, what two things are necessary for founding and maintaining a great empire? (2 pts.)

   5.1

   Old-fashioned men and ancient customs

2. According to Cicero, how did his generation treat the mos maiorum? (3 pts.)

   5.2

   Cicero's generation treated it like a magnificent picture which it refused to restore, and neglected until the original could hardly be seen.

3. According to Cicero, why had Rome lost the name and substance of Republic? (1 pt.)

   5.2

   Moral failings

4. According to Scipio, in what two aspects of law does a statesman need to be versed? (2 pts.)

   5.5

   The fundamental principles; civil law

5. "No honest man can be corrupted by___a bribe___, but he *can* be corrupted by ___eloquence (5.11)___." (2 pts.)

THE REPUBLIC: Lesson 11 Quiz

Name:_____ Date: _____ Score: _____

13 pts.

1. According to Africanus, what happens to good statesmen when they die? (2 pts.)

   _____

   _____

   _____

2. According to Paulus, what way of life leads to heaven? (2 pts.)

   _____

   _____

   _____

3. According to Paulus, where do souls (of good men) live when released from their bodies? (1 pt.)

   _____

   _____

   _____

4. To what does Africanus compare the sun? (1 pt.)

   _____

   _____

   _____

5. According to Africanus, what is a man's "true self"? (1 pt.)

   _____

   _____

6. According to Africanus, what is mortal and what is immortal? (4 pts.)

   _____

   _____

   _____

   _____

7. According to Africanus, what causes death? (1 pt.)

   _____

   _____

   _____

8. On what grounds does Africanus assert that the mind is eternal? (1 pt.)

   _____

   _____

   _____

THE REPUBLIC: Lesson 11 Quiz – KEY

Name:_____ Date: _____ Score: _____

13 pts.

1. According to Africanus, what happens to good statesmen when they die? (2 pts.)
    6.13

    They have a place in heaven and enjoy a life of eternal bliss.

    _____

2. According to Paulus, what way of life leads to heaven? (2 pts.)
    6.16

    Respecting justice and doing your duty.

    _____

3. According to Paulus, where do souls (of good men) live when released from their bodies? (1 pt.)
    6.16

    The Milky Way

    _____

4. To what does Africanus compare the sun? (1 pt.)
    6.17

    To the statesman.

    _____

5. According to Africanus, what is a man's "true self"? (1 pt.)
    6.26

    His mind

    _____

6. According to Africanus, what is mortal and what is immortal? (4 pts.)
    6.26

    The soul and God are immortal.

    The body and the Universe are mortal.

    _____

7. According to Africanus, what causes death? (1 pt.)
    6.27

    The cessation of motion

    _____

8. On what grounds does Africanus assert that the mind is eternal? (1 pt.)
    6.28

    It moves itself.

    _____

THE REPUBLIC: Exam

Name:_____ Date: _____ Score: _____

100 pts.

PARTICIPANTS IN THE DIALOGUE (5 pts.)

1. _____ a legal expert

2. _____ Scipio's nephew and an eager student of philosophy

3. _____ a man of great personal rectitude who nevertheless takes on the defense of injustice for the sake of argument

4. _____ the destroyer of Carthage; an extraordinary general who did not threaten the state as the great generals of Cicero's time did

5. _____ conservative, anti-democracy

COMPREHENSION QUESTIONS (45 pts.)

6. Why is law superior to philosophy? (2 pts.)

_____

_____

_____

_____

7. Why was Scipio impressed by Galus? (2 pts.)

_____

_____

_____

_____

_____

8. Who does Scipio believe is the worst kind of person? (1 pt.)

_____

_____

_____

9. How does Scipio define the common law of nature regarding possessions? (1 pt.)

_____

_____

_____

_____

10. What does Laelius say Scipio believed to be the best condition of the state? (1 pt.)

_____

_____

_____

11. Which form of government does Scipio say is least desirable? (1 pt.)

_____

_____

_____

12. What kind of government does Scipio say is most to be desired? (1 pt.)

_____

_____

_____

13. How does discord arise in a state? (2 pts.)

_____

_____

_____

14. What holds a community of citizens together? (2 pts.)

_____

_____

_____

15. Why does Scipio say it is hard to choose which system of government is best? (6 pts.)

_____

_____

_____

16. Who received the plunder from Romulus's wars? (2 pts.)

_____

_____

_____

17. What things provide the most favorable conditions for the growth of justice and good faith? (2 pts.)

_____

_____

_____

18. How did Servius Tullius rearrange the Assemblies to take power away from the people? (2 pts.)

_____

_____

_____

_____

19. Who are the assidui? (1 pt.)

_____

_____

_____

20. Who are the proletarii? (1 pt.)

_____

_____

_____

21. How does Scipio define freedom? (2 pts.)

_____

_____

_____

22. Why did the people initially put up with Tarquinius Superbus even though he was harsh and unjust? (2 pts.)

_____

_____

_____

23. To preserve a government from change, the magistrates must have _____, the

aristocratic council _____, and the people _____. (3 pts.)

24. According the Philus, what is the simplest way of getting at the truth? (1 pt.)

_____

_____

_____

25. According to Philus, how would things be different if justice were a function of nature? (2 pts.)

_____

_____

_____

_____

26. According to Philus, what causes the compromise of mixed government? (2 pts.)

_____

_____

_____

27. "No honest man can be corrupted by_____, but he _can_ be corrupted by

_____." (2 pts.)

28. According to Africanus, what is mortal and what is immortal? (4 pts.)

_____

_____

_____

_____

ESSAYS (50 pts.)

Answer two of the questions below in short essays of a page or less for 25 points each. Keep in mind that there are no simple right or wrong philosophical opinions. Craft a thorough, thoughtful argument, and be sure to consider diverse philosophical perspectives and rationally address counterarguments. Emphasis for grading purposes will be placed on critical thinking, logical organization, and thorough dialectic.

1. Does education imply greater obligation to the state?

2. Scipio seems to believe that some people are just naturally better than others, and to treat everyone equally is, then, unfair. Bear in mind that this belief is based on men's natures, not their actions. Do you agree with Scipio's assessment of the stratification of human goodness? Why or why not? What are the political and legal implications of your opinion?

3. Much of Scipio's support for monarchy rests on his implicit assumption that leading the state is a specialized task that requires specialists (hence the doctor and captain analogy), and therefore cannot be properly carried out by anyone else. Do you agree? Why or why not?

4. Philus asserts that justice is political rather than natural, and Laelius argues that justice is a function of natural (and universal) law. Which do you think is more likely and why? Be sure to refute the arguments of the other side.

5. Much of Book III discusses the relationship between legality and justice. What do you perceive this relationship to be?

Student Essays:

_____

_____

_____

_____

_____

_____

THE REPUBLIC: Exam – KEY

Name:_____ Date: _____ Score: _____

100 pts.

PARTICIPANTS IN THE DIALOGUE (5 pts.)

1. __Manilius__ a legal expert

2. __Tubero__ Scipio's nephew and an eager student of philosophy

3. __Philus__ a man of great personal rectitude who nevertheless takes on the defense of injustice for the sake of argument

4. __Scipio__ the destroyer of Carthage; an extraordinary general who did not threaten the state as the great generals of Cicero's time did

5. __Mummius__ conservative, anti-democracy

COMPREHENSION QUESTIONS (45 pts.)

6. Why is law superior to philosophy? (2 pts.)

   1.3

   The law compels everyone to do what philosophy can persuade only a few people to do.

7. Why was Scipio impressed by Galus? (2 pts.)

   1.23

   Galus had been able to convince the troops to set aside their fear at an eclipse by explaining it as a natural and scientific phenomenon rather than a portent of ill luck from the gods.

8. Who does Scipio believe is the worst kind of person? (1 pt.)

   1.27

   Often the worst kind of person has possessions and power in limitless quantities.

9. How does Scipio define the common law of nature regarding possessions? (1 pt.)

1.27

It forbids anything to belong to anyone except someone who knows how to employ and use it.

10. What does Laelius say Scipio believed to be the best condition of the state? (1 pt.)

1.34

The one handed down by the ancestors.

11. Which form of government does Scipio say is least desirable? (1 pt.)

1.42

Rule by the people

12. What kind of government does Scipio say is most to be desired? (1 pt.)

1.45

One that is blended from the three basic types (monarchy, democracy, oligarchy).

13. How does discord arise in a state? (2 pts.)

1.49

It arises from incompatible interests, when different policies suit different people.

14. What holds a community of citizens together? (2 pts.)

1.49

Equality under the law

15. Why does Scipio say it is hard to choose which system of government is best? (6 pts.)

1.55

- Kings attract us by affection.
- Aristocracies attract us by good sense.
- Democracies attract us by freedom.

16. Who received the plunder from Romulus's wars? (2 pts.)

2.15

Only the citizens, not Romulus himself.

17. What things provide the most favorable conditions for the growth of justice and good faith? (2 pts.)

2.26

Peace and relaxation

18. How did Servius Tullius rearrange the Assemblies to take power away from the people? (2 pts.)

2.39

He organized them into five classes, and distributed them in such a way that most votes were in the hands of the wealthy.

19. Who are the assidui? (1 pt.)

2.40

The rich

20. Who are the proletarii? (1 pt.)

2.40

The poor

21. How does Scipio define freedom? (2 pts.)

2.43

Having no master at all, even a just one.

22. Why did the people initially put up with Tarquinius Superbus even though he was harsh and unjust? (2 pts.)

2.44

His military success brought wealth into Rome.

23. To preserve a government from change, the magistrates must have ___adequate power___, the aristocratic council ___adequate influence___, and the people ___adequate freedom (2.57)___. (3 pts.)

24. According the Philus, what is the simplest way of getting at the truth? (1 pt.)

3.8

Arguing both sides of a case.

25. According to Philus, how would things be different if justice were a function of nature? (2 pts.)

3.18

Every country would have the same laws, and one country would not have different laws at different times.

26. According to Philus, what causes the compromise of mixed government? (2 pts.)

3.23

Mutual fear between classes and individuals.

27. "No honest man can be corrupted by _____a bribe_____, but he *can* be corrupted by _____eloquence (5.11)_____." (2 pts.)

28. According to Africanus, what is mortal and what is immortal? (4 pts.)

6.26

The soul and God are immortal.

The body and the Universe are mortal.

ESSAYS (50 pts.)

Answer two of the questions below in short essays of a page or less for 25 points each. Keep in mind that there are no simple right or wrong philosophical opinions. Craft a thorough, thoughtful argument, and be sure to consider diverse philosophical perspectives and rationally address counterarguments. Emphasis for grading purposes will be placed on critical thinking, logical organization, and thorough dialectic.

1. Does education imply greater obligation to the state?

2. Scipio seems to believe that some people are just naturally better than others, and to treat everyone equally is, then, unfair. Bear in mind that this belief is based on men's natures, not their actions. Do you agree with Scipio's assessment of the stratification of human goodness? Why or why not? What are the political and legal implications of your opinion?

3. Much of Scipio's support for monarchy rests on his implicit assumption that leading the state is a specialized task that requires specialists (hence the doctor and captain analogy), and therefore cannot be properly carried out by anyone else. Do you agree? Why or why not?

4. Philus asserts that justice is political rather than natural, and Laelius argues that justice is a function of natural (and universal) law. Which do you think is more likely and why? Be sure to refute the arguments of the other side.

5. Much of Book III discusses the relationship between legality and justice. What do you perceive this relationship to be?

THE LAWS: Lesson 12 Quiz

Name:_____ Date: _____ Score: _____

31 pts.

1. _____ our author's younger brother (2 pts.)

2. _____ Titus Pomponius Atticus, Cicero's lifelong friend. He lived in Athens and was an Epicurean. (2 pts.)

3. _____ the author of this work (2 pts.)

4. Why does Cicero inquire about the legends of Quirinus and Orithyia? (2 pts.)

_____

_____

_____

_____

5. What two kinds of truth does Cicero explain? (2 pts.)

_____

_____

_____

6. From what does Cicero believe law to be derived? (2 pts.)

_____

_____

_____

7. What does Cicero claim will guide his discussion of the origins of justice? (1 pt.)

_____

_____

_____

8. Summarize Cicero's argument that men are the partners of the gods in law. (3 pts.)

_____

_____

_____

_____

_____

9. According to Cicero, how can the universe be considered a single community shared by gods and men? (3 pts.)

_____

_____

_____

_____

10. To what does Cicero attribute individual differences between people? (3 pts.)

_____

_____

_____

_____

11. What does Cicero believe about the nature of vice? (3 pts.)

_____

_____

_____

_____

12. According to Cicero, why are those who receive public honors considered blessed and the obscure pitied? (1 pt.)

_____

_____

_____

13. According to Cicero, what do all communities reject and hate? (2 pts.)

_____

_____

_____

14. According to Cicero, how has nature given justice to mankind? (2 pts.)

_____

_____

_____

15. What did Socrates claim was the source of everything pernicious? (1 pt.)

_____

_____

_____

THE LAWS: Lesson 12 Quiz – KEY

Name:_____ Date: _____ Score: _____

31 pts.

1. __Quintus_____ our author's younger brother (2 pts.)

2. __Atticus_____ Titus Pomponius Atticus, Cicero's lifelong friend. He lived in Athens and was an Epicurean. (2 pts.)

3. __Marcus_____ the author of this work (2 pts.)

4. Why does Cicero inquire about the legends of Quirinus and Orithyia? (2 pts.)
   1.4
   Cicero inquires to make a point about respecting mythological tradition for its own sake rather than examining it for literal truth.

5. What two kinds of truth does Cicero explain? (2 pts.)
   1.5
   Historical truth and poetic truth (which is meant to entertain).

6. From what does Cicero believe law to be derived? (2 pts.)
   1.17
   From philosophy rather than civil law or precedent.

7. What does Cicero claim will guide his discussion of the origins of justice? (1 pt.)
   1.20
   Nature

8. Summarize Cicero's argument that men are the partners of the gods in law. (3 pts.)
   1.23
   Men and gods share reason.
   Reason is the law.
   Ergo men and gods share the law.

9. According to Cicero, how can the universe be considered a single community shared by gods and men? (3 pts.)

1.23

Men and gods share justice in law, ergo they share the same state. Moreover, they are all subject to the same authority, an all-powerful god.

10. To what does Cicero attribute individual differences between people? (3 pts.)

1.29

We are naturally identical, but corrupt habits and foolish opinions twist and turn our feeble minds from their original paths.

11. What does Cicero believe about the nature of vice? (3 pts.)

1.31

Pleasure leads to vice. Pleasure resembles what is naturally good, so through it vice can be mistakenly accepted as something beneficial.

12. According to Cicero, why are those who receive public honors considered blessed and the obscure pitied? (1 pt.)

1.32

Because good character and good reputation look alike.

13. According to Cicero, what do all communities reject and hate? (2 pts.)

1.32

The arrogant, the wicked, the cruel, and the ungrateful.

14. According to Cicero, how has nature given justice to mankind? (2 pts.)

1.33

Nature has endowed us with reason, hence right reason, hence law, hence justice.

15. What did Socrates claim was the source of everything pernicious? (1 pt.)

1.33

The separation of self-interest from justice.

THE LAWS: Lesson 13 Quiz

Name:_____ Date: _____ Score: _____

12 pts.

1. According to Cicero, under what conditions does society lose the distinction between the just and the unjust? (2 pts.)

   _____

   _____

   _____

   _____

2. According to Cicero, how would a good man and an advantage-seeking man act toward a helpless rich stranger met on the road? (3 pts.)

   _____

   _____

   _____

   _____

3. According to Cicero, what is most foolish of all? (1 pt.)

   _____

   _____

   _____

4. What is Cicero's justification for saying some laws of nations are unjust? (2 pts.)

   _____

   _____

   _____

5. According to Cicero, what is goodness sought for its own advantages? (1 pt.)

   _____

   _____

   _____

6. What does Cicero assert the law should do? (2 pts.)

   _____

   _____

   _____

7. What most difficult lesson does wisdom teach? (1 pt.)

   _____

   _____

   _____

THE LAWS: Lesson 13 Quiz – KEY

Name:_____ Date: _____ Score: _____

12 pts.

1. According to Cicero, under what conditions does society lose the distinction between the just and the unjust? (2 pts.)

   1.40

   When it is the fear of punishment that deters people from crime rather than distaste for wickedness.

2. According to Cicero, how would a good man and an advantage-seeking man act toward a helpless rich stranger met on the road? (3 pts.)

   1.41

   The good man helps him, and the advantage-seeking man either kills him and robs him, or refrains from it only because he is afraid of being found out and punished.

3. According to Cicero, what is most foolish of all? (1 pt.)

   1.42

   The belief that everything decreed by institutions or laws of a particular country is just.

4. What is Cicero's justification for saying some laws of nations are unjust? (2 pts.)

   1.42

   They are opposed to natural justice and natural law.

5. According to Cicero, what is goodness sought for its own advantages? (1 pt.)

   1.49

   Selfishness

6. What does Cicero assert the law should do? (2 pts.)

   1.58

   Correct wickedness and promote goodness.

7. What most difficult lesson does wisdom teach? (1 pt.)

   1.58

   To know ourselves.

THE LAWS: Lesson 14 Quiz

Name:_____ Date: _____ Score: _____

10 pts.

1. According to Cicero, on what must laws be founded? (1 pt.)

    _____

    _____

    _____

2. According to Cicero, from where does law *not* come? (2 pts.)

    _____

    _____

    _____

3. According to Cicero, what is the original and final law? (2 pts.)

    _____

    _____

    _____

4. According to Cicero, what should be the measure of whether a law is just or unjust? (1 pt.)

    _____

    _____

    _____

5. How did Plato believe laws should be accepted? (2 pts.)

    _____

    _____

    _____

6. According to Cicero's laws, what should be worshiped in addition to the gods? (2 pts.)

    _____

    _____

    _____

THE LAWS: Lesson 14 Quiz – KEY

Name:_____ Date: _____ Score: _____

10 pts.

1. According to Cicero, on what must laws be founded? (1 pt.)
   2.8
   _____

   Reason
   _____

   _____

2. According to Cicero, from where does law *not* come? (2 pts.)
   2.8
   _____

   Not from the intelligence of human beings, or from resolutions passed by communities.
   _____

   _____

3. According to Cicero, what is the original and final law? (2 pts.)
   2.8
   _____

   The intelligence of God, who ordains or forbids everything by reason.
   _____

   _____

4. According to Cicero, what should be the measure of whether a law is just or unjust? (1 pt.)
   2.13
   _____

   Nature
   _____

   _____

5. How did Plato believe laws should be accepted? (2 pts.)
   2.14
   _____

   By consent rather than threats of violence.
   _____

   _____

6. According to Cicero's laws, what should be worshiped in addition to the gods? (2 pts.)
   2.19
   _____

   Men who have become gods and the qualities that allow men to become gods.
   _____

   _____

THE LAWS: Lesson 15 Quiz

Name:_____ Date: _____ Score: _____

11 pts.

1. What is Cicero's objection to foreign gods and new gods? (2 pts.)

    _____

    _____

    _____

2. Why does Cicero, a Skeptic and follower of Plato, believe in divination? (4 pts.)

    _____

    _____

    _____

    _____

    _____

3. According to Cicero, what should be the most important factors in all aspects of a war? (2 pts.)

    _____

    _____

    _____

4. What does Cicero find disturbing about the contemporary music of his day? (1 pt.)

    _____

    _____

    _____

5. Why does Cicero believe pontiffs should not be involved in or knowledgeable of civil law? (2 pts.)

    _____

    _____

    _____

    _____

THE LAWS: Lesson 15 Quiz – KEY

Name:_____ Date: _____ Score: _____

11 pts.

1. What is Cicero's objection to foreign gods and new gods? (2 pts.)

   2.25-2.26

   They cause confusion because the rites are unfamiliar.

2. Why does Cicero, a Skeptic and follower of Plato, believe in divination? (4 pts.)

   2.32-2.33

   1 - Logic: The gods are real; they rule the world; they have the power to give signs;
   they care for mankind.

   2 - He claims history bears out the predictions of past augurs.

3. According to Cicero, what should be the most important factors in all aspects of a war? (2 pts.)

   2.34

   Justice and good faith

4. What does Cicero find disturbing about the contemporary music of his day? (1 pt.)

   2.39

   People swaying and nodding their heads in time with the music.

5. Why does Cicero believe pontiffs should not be involved in or knowledgeable of civil law? (2 pts.)

   2.52-2.53

   Because they can use it to circumvent religious authority and obligations (for example,
   the rites of the deceased).

THE LAWS: Lesson 16 Quiz

Name:_____ Date: _____ Score: _____

15 pts.

1. What powers does Cicero reserve for all magistrates? (3 pts.)

    _____

    _____

    _____

2. According to Cicero, who should appoint the magistrates? (1 pt.)

    _____

    _____

3. According to Cicero, how should meetings of the senate be conducted? (5 pts.)

    _____

    _____

    _____

    _____

4. Why does Quintus call the birth of the tribunate "a great calamity"? (2 pts.)

    _____

    _____

    _____

5. Why does Marcus disagree with Quintus? (2 pts.)

    _____

    _____

    _____

6. What does Cicero assert is the primary problem with aristocratic corruption? (1 pt.)

    _____

    _____

    _____

7. To what does Plato attribute changes in the nature of the state? (1 pt.)

    _____

    _____

    _____

THE LAWS: Lesson 16 Quiz – KEY

Name:_____ Date: _____ Score: _____

15 pts.

1. What powers does Cicero reserve for all magistrates? (3 pts.)

   3.10

   The right to take auspices, conduct trials, and veto the decrees of lower magistrates.

2. According to Cicero, who should appoint the magistrates? (1 pt.)

   3.10

   The people

3. According to Cicero, how should meetings of the senate be conducted? (5 pts.)

   3.10-3.11

   They should be conducted with decent restraint. Senators should be punished for
   unexcused absences. Senators must speak in turn and briefly. They should have a
   grasp of public affairs.

4. Why does Quintus call the birth of the tribunate "a great calamity"? (2 pts.)

   3.17

   Because it took power from the aristocracy and empowered the people.

5. Why does Marcus disagree with Quintus? (2 pts.)

   3.17

   Because unchecked consular power appears arrogant and oppressive.

6. What does Cicero assert is the primary problem with aristocratic corruption? (1 pt.)

   3.31

   It leads to corruption in the other classes as well.

7. To what does Plato attribute changes in the nature of the state? (1 pt.)

   3.32

   Changes in the vocal style of its musicians.

THE LAWS: Lesson 17 Quiz

Name:_____ Date: _____ Score: _____

15 pts.

1. According to Cicero, what three things should be required of senators? (3 pts.)

   _____

   _____

   _____

   _____

2. Under what circumstances does Cicero approve of long speeches? (2 pts.)

   _____

   _____

   _____

   _____

3. According to Cicero, with what knowledge does a senator need to be equipped for his job? (9 pts.)

   _____

   _____

   _____

   _____

   _____

   _____

4. Why does Cicero claim *privilegia* are unjust? (1 pt.)

   _____

   _____

   _____

THE LAWS: Lesson 17 Quiz – KEY

Name:_____ Date: _____ Score: _____

15 pts.

1. According to Cicero, what three things should be required of senators? (3 pts.)

   3.40

   That they be present at meetings of the senate; that they speak in turn; that they be brief.

2. Under what circumstances does Cicero approve of long speeches? (2 pts.)

   3.40

   When the senate is going wrong and no one is attempting to save the situation; when an issue is exceptionally important.

3. According to Cicero, with what knowledge does a senator need to be equipped for his job? (9 pts.)

   3.41

   Know the state of the country regarding troops, finances, allies, tributaries, laws, conditions, treaties; understand legislative procedure; be aware of the traditional precedent.

4. Why does Cicero claim *privilegia* are unjust? (1 pt.)

   3.44

   By definition, a law is something that applies to everyone.

THE LAWS: Exam

Name:_____ Date: _____ Score: _____
100 pts.

PARTICIPANTS IN THE DIALOGUE (3 pts.)

1. _____ our author's younger brother

2. _____ Titus Pomponius Atticus, Cicero's lifelong friend. He lived in Athens and was an Epicurean.

3. _____ the author of this work

COMPREHENSION QUESTIONS (45 pts.)

4. What two kinds of truth does Cicero explain? (2 pts.)

_____

_____

_____

5. From what does Cicero believe law to be derived? (2 pts.)

_____

_____

_____

6. What does Cicero claim will guide his discussion of the origins of justice? (1 pt.)

_____

_____

_____

7. What does Cicero believe about the nature of vice? (3 pts.)

_____

_____

_____

_____

8. According to Cicero, how has nature given justice to mankind? (2 pts.)

_____

_____

_____

9. What did Socrates claim was the source of everything pernicious? (1 pt.)

_____

_____

_____

10. According to Cicero, under what conditions does society lose the distinction between the just and the unjust? (2 pts.)

_____

_____

_____

11. According to Cicero, how would a good man and an advantage-seeking man act toward a helpless rich stranger met on the road? (3 pts.)

_____

_____

_____

_____

12. According to Cicero, what is most foolish of all? (1 pt.)

_____

_____

_____

13. What is Cicero's justification for saying some laws of nations are unjust? (2 pts.)

_____

_____

_____

14. According to Cicero, what is goodness sought for its own advantages? (1 pt.)

_____

_____

_____

15. What does Cicero assert the law should do? (2 pts.)

_____

_____

_____

16. What most difficult lesson does wisdom teach? (1 pt.)

_____

_____

_____

17. According to Cicero, on what must laws be founded? (1 pt.)

_____

_____

_____

18. How did Plato believe laws should be accepted? (2 pts.)

_____

_____

_____

19. According to Cicero, what should be the most important factors in all aspects of a war? (2 pts.)

_____

_____

_____

20. According to Cicero, how should meetings of the senate be conducted? (5 pts.)

_____

_____

_____

_____

21. Why does Quintus call the birth of the tribunate "a great calamity"? (2 pts.)

_____

_____

_____

22. Under what circumstances does Cicero approve of long speeches? (2 pts.)

_____

_____

_____

_____

23. According to Cicero, with what knowledge does a senator need to be equipped for his job? (9 pts.)

_____

_____

_____

_____

_____

24. Why does Cicero claim _privilegia_ are unjust? (1 pt.)

_____

_____

_____

ESSAYS (50 pts.)

Answer two of the questions below in short essays of a page or less for 25 points each. Keep in mind that there are no simple right or wrong philosophical opinions. Craft a thorough, thoughtful argument, and be sure to consider diverse philosophical perspectives and rationally address counterarguments. Emphasis for grading purposes will be placed on critical thinking, logical organization, and thorough dialectic.

1. Cicero asserts that justice is a function of nature evident in all human societies. Write an argument that this is the case, and an argument that it isn't the case. Do not recycle Cicero's reasons.

2. What advantage might a man get out of helping another man? Is that action still good? Does a self-serving motivation nullify the goodness of an action, or are actions good or bad independent of motivations? If it does nullify it, to what extent does it do so?

3. Cicero asserts that some rules laid down by societies are just (and therefore true) laws, and some are unjust (and therefore undeserving of the name of law), but he does not address how a person should act who does not live in his utopia of perfectly just civil law. Let us assume that some of our laws are just and some unjust. Should citizens obey unjust laws? Come up with three reasons and one scenario to support each side of this question.

4. Cicero's laws require magistrates leaving office to make a report and account for their actions in office. Why would this be a good practice? Why would this be a harmful practice? Be sure to address both sides of this issue.

Student Essays:

_____

_____

_____

_____

_____

_____

_____

_____

_____

_____

_____

_____

_____

_____

_____

_____

_____

THE LAWS: Exam – KEY

Name:_____ Date: _____ Score: _____

100 pts.

PARTICIPANTS IN THE DIALOGUE (3 pts.)

1. <u>Quintus</u> our author's younger brother

2. <u>Atticus</u> Titus Pomponius Atticus, Cicero's lifelong friend. He lived in Athens and was an Epicurean.

3. <u>Marcus</u> the author of this work

COMPREHENSION QUESTIONS (45 pts.)

4. What two kinds of truth does Cicero explain? (2 pts.)

   1.5

   Historical truth and poetic truth (which is meant to entertain).

5. From what does Cicero believe law to be derived? (2 pts.)

   1.17

   From philosophy rather than civil law or precedent.

6. What does Cicero claim will guide his discussion of the origins of justice? (1 pt.)

   1.20

   Nature

7. What does Cicero believe about the nature of vice? (3 pts.)

   1.31

   Pleasure leads to vice. Pleasure resembles what is naturally good, so through it vice can be mistakenly accepted as something beneficial.

8. According to Cicero, how has nature given justice to mankind? (2 pts.)

   1.33

   Nature has endowed us with reason, hence right reason, hence law, hence justice.

9. What did Socrates claim was the source of everything pernicious? (1 pt.)

1.33

The separation of self-interest from justice.

10. According to Cicero, under what conditions does society lose the distinction between the just and the unjust? (2 pts.)

1.40

When it is the fear of punishment that deters people from crime rather than distaste for wickedness.

11. According to Cicero, how would a good man and an advantage-seeking man act toward a helpless rich stranger met on the road? (3 pts.)

1.41

The good man helps him, and the advantage-seeking man either kills him and robs him, or refrains from it only because he is afraid of being found out and punished.

12. According to Cicero, what is most foolish of all? (1 pt.)

1.42

The belief that everything decreed by institutions or laws of a particular country is just.

13. What is Cicero's justification for saying some laws of nations are unjust? (2 pts.)

1.42

They are opposed to natural justice and natural law.

14. According to Cicero, what is goodness sought for its own advantages? (1 pt.)

1.49

Selfishness

15. What does Cicero assert the law should do? (2 pts.)

1.58

Correct wickedness and promote goodness.

16. What most difficult lesson does wisdom teach? (1 pt.)

1.58

To know ourselves.

17. According to Cicero, on what must laws be founded? (1 pt.)

2.8

Reason

18. How did Plato believe laws should be accepted? (2 pts.)

2.14

By consent rather than threats of violence.

19. According to Cicero, what should be the most important factors in all aspects of a war? (2 pts.)

2.34

Justice and good faith

20. According to Cicero, how should meetings of the senate be conducted? (5 pts.)

3.10-3.11

They should be conducted with decent restraint. Senators should be punished for unexcused absences. Senators must speak in turn and briefly. They should have a grasp of public affairs.

21. Why does Quintus call the birth of the tribunate "a great calamity"? (2 pts.)

3.17

Because it took power from the aristocracy and empowered the people.

22. Under what circumstances does Cicero approve of long speeches? (2 pts.)

3.40

When the senate is going wrong and no one is attempting to save the situation; when an issue is exceptionally important.

23. According to Cicero, with what knowledge does a senator need to be equipped for his job? (9 pts.)

3.41

Know the state of the country regarding troops, finances, allies, tributaries, laws, conditions, treaties; understand legislative procedure; be aware of the traditional precedent.

24. Why does Cicero claim *privilegia* are unjust? (1 pt.)

3.44

By definition, a law is something that applies to everyone.

ESSAYS (50 pts.)

Answer two of the questions below in short essays of a page or less for 25 points each. Keep in mind that there are no simple right or wrong philosophical opinions. Craft a thorough, thoughtful argument, and be sure to consider diverse philosophical perspectives and rationally address counterarguments. Emphasis for grading purposes will be placed on critical thinking, logical organization, and thorough dialectic.

1. Cicero asserts that justice is a function of nature evident in all human societies. Write an argument that this is the case, and an argument that it isn't the case. Do not recycle Cicero's reasons.

2. What advantage might a man get out of helping another man? Is that action still good? Does a self-serving motivation nullify the goodness of an action, or are actions good or bad independent of motivations? If it does nullify it, to what extent does it do so?

3. Cicero asserts that some rules laid down by societies are just (and therefore true) laws, and some are unjust (and therefore undeserving of the name of law), but he does not address how a person should act who does not live in his utopia of perfectly just civil law. Let us assume that some of our laws are just and some unjust. Should citizens obey unjust laws? Come up with three reasons and one scenario to support each side of this question.

4. Cicero's laws require magistrates leaving office to make a report and account for their actions in office. Why would this be a good practice? Why would this be a harmful practice? Be sure to address both sides of this issue.

Made in the USA
Charleston, SC
25 March 2014